Walks Thro' Coventry 1916

(Illustrated)

Edwin Rainbow/

Foreword and illustrations
by
Paula Jeffery

Harefield Press

Published by: Harefield Press

Text Design: Paula Jeffery

Cover Design: Paula Jeffery

ISBN-13: 978-1-9998087-0-9

Dedicated to my late grandfather
Len Rainbow, a kind, intelligent and
thoughtful man who probably missed his
own grandfather as much as I miss mine.

Foreword

I never met Edwin Rainbow but I knew a man who did.

Edwin was the beloved grandfather of my own lovely grandfather, Leonard Rainbow. Len was 12 years old in 1918 when Edwin died suddenly at the age of 66. He had been close to Edwin - the extended family had lived in the same house - and the shock of his early death effected Len deeply. He always spoke with affection about his grandfather and talked of how Edwin would take him into Coventry city centre and what an impressive sight he was with his top hat and pocket watch on a gold chain.

Len died in 2000, aged 94 and I wish I'd asked him more about Edwin. Although I've found out about many aspects of my great, great grandfather's life, probably much more than Len knew about him, I know few personal details.

He was born in 1851 in High Street, Coventry the son of silk weavers. By the time he was ten the city was hit by hard times as the silk weaving industry began a rapid and dramatic decline. Such was the devastation that a national fund was organised to send relief and many people left the area or emigrated.

However, Edwin's parents, James and Sarah stayed and Edwin attended Bablake School, leaving at 15 to train as a printer's apprentice. He went on to work for several Coventry newspapers and eventually became a journalist. He later became Registrar for Births and Deaths in the city and was involved, as Secretary, in numerous local institutions including the Coventry School of Art and the Coventry Technical Institute.

Towards the end of his life he developed a passion for Bohemia and wrote articles for national newspapers describing his trips. The freedom of Prague was conferred upon him in recognition of his services in disseminating information concerning that country . However, he didn't neglect his own country and home town. He wrote the official guides for the celebration of Queen Victoria's Golden and Diamond Jubilees and this book, Walks Thro' Coventry was published in 1916.

It would appear that this version of 'Walks' was based on an 1888 book published by Caldicott and rewritten by Edwin. Much of the material relates to the changes that had taken place in Coventry in the preceding twenty five years.

As Edwin gives us a tour of the city centre, road by road mentioning the benefactors and businesses along the way we are reminded of gracious tree lined avenues and sparse traffic in a time before Coventry was decimated by the Blitz, when all its historic grandeur remained largely intact.

Walks Thro' Coventry gives a unique insight into a city at the turn of the 20th century with Edwin exploring the past but also expounding on the progress the city had made and its hopes for the future.

I'm re-publishing this guide in Edwin's memory and, knowing of his passion for technological advancements and further education, in the knowledge that he would almost certainly approve.

Paula Jeffery

Contents

List of Illustrations

Edwin Rainbow
1851–1918

Introduction

"Welcome every smiles" - Shakespeare

Coventry enjoys the distinction of being the central city of England; it is equi-distant from sea to sea, except due north. There are three reputed "centres of England," each being about eight miles away in different direction. But Coventry has more solid claims to world-wide fame than its geographical situation, as closer acquaintance reveals.

We will presume the visitor to our ancient and interesting city has arrived by railway, and having given him a cordial greeting we will engage his attention with a few general remarks, prior to our perambulations.

In one respect Coventry is not to be envied. Although several railways run through the neighbourhood - the Great Western within ten miles, and the Great Central within twelve - this now important city is bound to one: the London and North-Western, plus any advantage that results from its practical amalgamation with the Midland Railway. Its station is on the London to Birmingham line, being 94 miles from the Metropolis and 18 1/2 miles from Birmingham. There are branch lines running to Leamington in one direction and Nuneaton in the other. On the whole, however, the London and North-Western may be said to afford the utmost facilities which are within the power of any one company. The station is only a short distance from the heart of the city, a little to the east of Warwick Road, and has lately been enlarged and made more convenient.

Leaving the Railway Station and proceeding towards the city, we enter Eaton Road, a modern thoroughfare named after a former M.P. for Coventry, afterwards Lord Cheylesmore, over whose land the road was constructed. There will first be noticed the floral and horticultural establishments of Mr. John Stevens, part of whose nurseries lie to the left. At this point, also, is the terminus of

The Electric Tramways

The lines run from the Railway station through the centre of the city to Foleshill and Bedworth on the north east, and have branches to the districts of Hillfields, Stoke, and the Stoney Stanton Road as far as Bell Green, and other branches to Chapel Fields and Earlsdon via Spon Street. Since 1st January 1912, the whole system has been the property of the Coventry Corporation.

By reason of narrowness of the streets a single track only is used, consequently the service is not wholly satisfactory and sufficient, although the Manager and Tramway Committee deserve credit for making the best use of the plant at their command.

The station for generating electrical energy is on Stoney Stanton Road, whence the whole system receives its supply of electricity. The cars are lighted both inside and outside by electricity.

At the end of Eaton Road we will turn left (passing the conservatories of Messrs. Perkins and Sons on the right), and, proceeding up the Warwick Road a short distance beyond the railway bridge, reach the "Top Green," a pleasant enclosed promenade, where lawn tennis and other light games may be played. The handsome buildings on the right are those of KING HENRY VIII SCHOOL, which was erected in 1885, at a cost of about £21,000, and are constructed of Woodville red brick, with Ancaster stone dressings. The main entrance is in the centre of the building, which at the south end has the head master's house. The school was founded by John Hales, in the reign to Henry VIII, hence its name, and, until the erection of the present buildings, was conducted in the Old Grammer School, Hales Street, an ancient structure, formerly known as the Hospital of St. John the Baptist, naturally deficient in all the requirements of modern education. In the battlements of the tower surmounting the entrance to the building a shield is bearing the arms of Henry VIII, and under this is another panel carved with the motto of the school.

If we walk up this road for a short distance we come to Stivichall Grove, where there is "a parting of the way" - that is to the right leading by extensive common lands and a grand avenue to Kenilworth (five miles), and via Guy's Cliff to Warwick (ten miles); the road to the left leading through beautiful scenery, by the Parks of Stoneleigh, where is the seat of Lord Leigh, to the Royal Spa of Leamington (eight and a half miles). The drive in either direction is considered to be unsurpassed in England for sylvan beauty.

Returning to the railway bridge, recently considerably enlarged, we have an indication of the primitive accommodation originally thought to be sufficient for a station. Hereon, we may take our stand, like Tennyson, when, on the less spacious structure, he wrote⊠

"I waited for the train at Coventry;
I hung with grooms and porters on the bridge,
To watch the three tall spires; and there I shap'd
The city's ancient legend"…

and for a few moments review the chief characteristics of this well known county borough.
Many quaint scenes of the past rise before our vision. We think of the time of the when the old Mystery Plays were acted in the narrow streets of the city; when the White and Grey Friars peopled the monasteries; and of occasions when the Parliament of the realm made Coventry its meeting place. Our imagination calls up many striking events in the historic past of the city, and

we revel in the richness of the field thus opening up before us.

There is, of course, a great contrast between the busy commercial centre of today and the Coventry of Queen Margaret; but on the whole it may be said that the modern city is worthy of its traditions.

In 1642, Nehemiah Wharton, an officer in the Parliamentary forces, under the Earl of Essex, described Coventry as a "city environed with a wall, co-equal, if not exceeding that of London for breadth and height, and with gates and battlements, magnificent churches and stately streets, and abundant fountains of water; altogether a place very sweetly situate, and where there is no hint of venison." Some of these features have disappeared, others remain in part, but many are still in existence, and go far to justify the eulogium, whilst the modern developments, both material and picturesque, are both numerous and important.

The largest town in Warwickshire, with the exception of Birmingham, Coventry is almost surrounded by a wealth of amenities. The north-east side of the city, however, reaches nearly to the Warwickshire coalfield, and here, of course, the scenery is not so pleasing, though lovers of of the picturesque need not search in vain, and there is some compensating advantage in the contiguity of so extensive a supply of fuel.

It will be seen that, for a manufacturing centre, Coventry is clean and salubrious, and this happy condition is partly due to large percentage of the power used in various industries supplied by gas or electricity, and thus diminishing the smoke nuisance.

That the city is a decidedly healthy place is proved by the low death rate, which averages about 12 per 1,000, the mean age at death, about 39, having risen by 4 in twenty years.

Though to a great extent modernised, the town still contains a large number of curious old buildings, churches, halls, alms-houses, etc, with rare historical associations and legends.

On November 1st 1890, a portion of the suburban districts were absorbed into the municipal area, and a further extension took place on November 1st 1899, when parts of Foleshill and Stoke came within city boundaries. These extensions were rendered necessary by the rapid growth of the town during years of industrial and commercial prosperity, the surrounding districts have become essentially urban in character, and being, in all but name, actually parts of the city. At the present time further extension of the city boundaries are badly required. Large neigh-bouring areas, notably those adjacent o the Stoke, Foleshill and Hearsall Wards, are densely populated mainly by city workers. For many reasons it is desirable that these should be included in the city's population, and serious movements in this direction were maturing, but like many other activities were interrupted by the European War. In 1888, Coventry resumed its old status and title of a county, which had been in abeyance since 1842.

Manufactures - In the sixteenth and seventeenth centuries the staple trade was the manufacture of woollen goods, but early in the eighteenth century the weaving of ribbons was introduced, and soon became an important industry, there being in 1818 in Coventry and the surrounding district no less than 3,003 power looms, and 5,438 single hand looms. Over half a century ago, however, the ribbon trade began to decline, and during a period of great distress many citizens emigrated. But from those evil days the modern prosperity of the city may be distinctly traced - new trades then introduced being the germs of its industrial development.

The manufactures of the city are, indeed, most varied, the older industries of watch-making and ribbon weaving being now secondary to an extensive cycle and motor car industry. Coventry productions now include engineering, etc., woollen goods, hosiery, coach trimmings, textile sundries, iron and brass founding, printing, electrical engineering, and various subsidiary trades; while among the later additions are the manufacture of steam valves, silk textile fabrics, artificial, ordnance, and aircraft.

The watch trade has been established here for at least two hundred years. In 1727 a watch-maker was Mayor of Coventry. The trade gradually grew in importance, until about fifty years ago it was considered to be one of the two "staple" trades of the city, and gave employment to about 2,000 persons. About 1858, however, a depression set in, and keen competition with American and Switzerland having had to be met, the organised factory system and machine methods have largely displaced the former domestic workshops and individual handicraft.

The enormous growth of the cycle trade has been the great feature in the history of the city during the past fifty years. The world prac- tically owes the bicycle to Coventry. In the early seventies a small band of intelligent mechanics, by their inventive genius, laid the foundation of what has now become a great and almost world-wide industry. Coventry has the highest reputation for its cycles and motor cars, and no efforts are wanting to retain its pre-eminence.

Populations - The earliest intimation of the approximate popula- tion of Coventry is given by Dugdale, who states when the great Benedictine Monastery, for which the city was formerly famous, was at the zenith of its prosperity, the inhabitants numbered 15,000 - a populations which at the time was considered extraordinary. Indeed, by the roll-tax of 1377, in the notices which it contains of the population of all the principal towns, Coventry appears third on the list in point of magnitude, next to London; York and Bristol being the only two taking precedence of it.

After the fall of the monastery the glory of the city appears to have departed, and the inhabitants dwindled down at one time to 3,000. However, the foundations of a healthy and vigorous community were deeply laid, and the city regained - though gradually - tis position, not indeed as third or fourth in the kingdom, but as a large centre of population. Upon the taking of the first national census in 1801, three centuries after its decline, the city contained 16,049 inhabitants. The successive stages by which lost ground was recovered may be traced thus: In 1586, where there was an enumeration of the inhabitants on account of the scarcity of provisions, the total number returned was 6,502. Under the provisions, the total number returned was 6,502. Under the apprehension of a siege during the Civil War in 1643 between the Parliament and the King, the people were numbered, with the result that they were found to be 9,500. According to "Bradford Survey" taken about 1748-49, the population was 12,817, so that it had not even then by over 2,000 reached the highest point at which it previously stood. The second national census showed a population of 17,242 - an increase of about 1,200 - and at the census of 1821 the number had increased to 21,242. The population as enumerated at subsequent periods had been as follows:

1831 £27,298	1871 £37,670
1841 £31,042	1881 £42,111
1851 £36,812	1891 £52,720
1861 £40,396	1901 £69,878

The only decrease was between 1861 and 1871, when a falling off of nearly 3,000 was due to depression in the ribbon and watch trades.

In 1911 the enumerated population was 106,377—an increase of 36,399, or more than 52 per cent. To the population of the County Borough (Urban District) has to be added that of the parishes of St. Michael and Holy Trinity without (the Rural District of Coventry) within the Coventry Poor Law Union and the Parliamentary Borough, of 582—the grand total for "Greater Coventry" being 106,959. It is estimated that by the present year (1916) the total population had further increased by upwards of 10 per cent. The population may now be taken as bordering on 130,000.

The area of the city in acres is 4,147; the assessable rateable value as at 31st March, 1916, is £483,324. The number of voters on the burgess roll for 1914-15 is over 23,000, and on the Parliamentary Register over 20,000.

Government.—Among other things in its history on which Coventry prides itself is the fact that for nearly six centuries it has had a Mayor and Corporation. Still to be seen is the Charter granted by King Edward III, dated January 20th, 1344, conferring these privileges upon Coventry, which, even at that remote period, was remarkable for its opulence, prosperity, and notable institutions. Thus was constituted a regular and permanent municipal government, and Coventry has ever since borne the coveted title of "city. " The first municipal council numbered 12. It now numbers 48, viz. : 12 aldermen and 36 councillors, the latter representing twelve wards. Among other responsibilities of the Corporation are the streets, which total up to a length of over 60 miles.

A Board of Guardians administers the Poor Law, maintaining a workhouse, officially termed the London Road Institution, with accommodation for about 500 inmates, a large infirmary, and several scattered homes for children.

The interests of the community as regards primary education were for upwards of thirty years cared for mainly by a School Board, who, in relinquishing their work to a Committee under the Education Act, 1902, transferred eleven schools, having accommodation for 7,110. There are now 15 Council Schools, with accommodation for 14,195, and 11 non-provided schools with accommodation for 3,386, making a total of 17,581 places. Schemes for the building of two new schools and enlargement of two existing schools to provide 3,123 more places have been postponed until after the war. At several centres instruction is given in special subjects—cookery, 7; laundry and house-wifery, 6; housecraft, 2 ; manual training, 6; gardening, 2 ; and a school for mental defectives. There are likewise several evening Continuation Schools, which form a link between primary and higher education.

As to secondary education, a Technical Instruction Committee, appointed by the Corporation, formerly carried on the School of Art and the Technical Institute. There are also a Day School of Science for Boys (Bablake), the Grammar School, a Girls' Secondary School, and other educational institutions, conspic-uous among them being a Central Free Public Library, and several Branch Libraries, which are well administered and highly appreciated. By the Education Act of 1902 the City Council, acting through a committee of twenty-five members, fifteen of whom are members of the Council, became responsible for supplying or aiding the supply of the whole of the educational needs of the city.

The lighting of the city, both by gas and electricity, is in the hands of the Corporation. The old gas works in Hill Street have been superseded by new works of a very extensive character at Foleshill. The electricity works adjoin the district of Radford, and supply current for the arc lamps which illuminate the central streets, and also for the numerous incandescent lamps used by tradesmen and private citizens.   The Gas Department has for many years yielded a profit for the reduction of the local rates, and the electricity undertaking, after a somewhat troublous infancy, is also profitable to the ratepayers, and has of late years proved itself a magnificently managed concern, its percentage of profits being the largest in the Kingdom.

In religious matters the Church of England comes first as regards amount of accommodation, but the Congregationalists, Baptists, Wesleyan Methodists, and Roman Catholics are strongly represented, while several other denominations have also a footing in the city, including the Society of Friends, Primitive Methodists, Free Methodists, Salvation Army, Plymouth Brethren, Spiritualists, Christadelphians, and Unitarians.

For 600 years Coventry sent two representatives to Parliament, but at the re-distribution of seats in 1885 the city was deprived of one of its members. The Parliamentary Register includes the "freemen," who have qualified by serving seven years' apprenticeship to one and the same trade in the city, who possess a valuable estate bequeathed by Sir Thomas White, the proceeds of which are given in weekly allowances to the senior freemen, and are entitled to certain grazing rights on the common lands. There are also many charities connected with the city, under the management of the General Charities Trustees and other bodies.

With reference to the ancient historical connections of the city, it may be observed that in old documents its name has been variously written Coventre and Coventria, both of which are supposed to have been derived from a convent established here in the seventh century, of which St. Osburg was the Abbess. This convent was destroyed by fire in 1015, when Edric invaded Mercia. An ingenious probable derivation of the name of the city was given by the late Mr. Doggett, of Bristol, who stated that in olden times a tree was planted near to monasteries called the covin tree, where barter and exchange were carried on. As it is well known that a convent was situated here, we may assume

18

that there was a covin tree, and the name may hence have been derived. But, leaving conjecture, it is recorded that in the year 1043, during the reign of Edward the Confessor, Leofric, Earl of Mercia, and his Countess, Godiva, erected a monastery on the site of a former convent. This monastery they richly endowed with money and land, one-half of the town and twenty-four lordships being appropriated to it. Its interior, according to an old writer, was covered with precious metal, and among other treasures it included an arm of St. Augustine, with an inscription recording that "it was purchased by Agebnethus, Archbishop of Canterbury, in 1020, for the sum of one talent of silver and two hundred talents of gold, from the Pope of Rome."

Lady Godiva

At this time, if we are to credit the legendists, Leofric for some reason or other oppressed the people of the town with grievous taxes, on account of which they made many complaints to the Earl and his Countess. The latter was deeply moved by the sufferings of the people, and their relief was due to an act of great self-sacrifice on the part of the Countess Godiva herself, who was constrained to plead their cause with the stern old Earl. As Tennyson says :—

"She sought her lord, and found him where he strode
About the hall, among his dogs, alone,
His beard a foot before him, and his hair
A yard behind.
She told him of their tears,
And prayed him, 'if they pay this tax they starve.
Startled, and half-amazed, the Earl cried in scorn—
"You would not let your little finger ache
For such as these?"
The Countess replied, "But I would die."

According to tradition he laughed, and by St. Peter and St. Paul took

19

an oath, exclaiming

"O, ay, ay, ay, you talk!"

The Countess, however, still persisting, said—

"But prove me what it is I would not do."
Then, in keeping with the rough nature of his heart
and the times in which he lived,
he gave her this reply—
"Ride you naked through the town, And I repeal it "

The conditions were doubtless thought by Leofric to be impossible. Nevertheless, the Countess accepted them, and to set the people free, on a certain day she rode forth till she beheld

"The white-flower'd elder-thicket from the field
Gleam through the Gothic archways in the wall,
Then she rode back, clothed on with chastity."

And a charter of freedom from servitude, evil customs, and exactions was granted to the city by the Earl, and presented to the Countess, who thus

"took the tax away, And built herself an everlasting name."

It is in commemoration of this romantic episode that the far-famed Godiva Pageant is occasionally held in the streets of the city. The Mayor and Corporation used to join in the celebration, and it is also composed of representatives of royal and other historic personages, friendly societies, local industries, with trade devices, and so forth, the central figure of course being an impersonation of the noble Countess, whose clothing of chastity only is suggested as far as conforms with modern notions of propriety.

Peeping Tom

Whatever truth there may be in the legend of Lady Godiva — and she certainly is historic — the story of Peeping Tom

may be safely called more picturesque — even grotesque — than veracious. The old tale runs that - disobeying - the request of the Countess to the people that, as she rode forth, "no foot should pace the street, no eye look down" — one tailor did basely and artfully bore a hole through his shutters in order that he might take a peep at the charitable lady; but, in the words of Tennyson again,—

"His eyes, before they had their will, Were shrivell'd into darkness in his head, And dropped before him."

This tradition of Peeping Tom, we may note, is not mentioned by the early historians, it is an excrescence, and most likely was added as a kind of attraction in the reign of Charles II at the time of the "celebration of the freedom of City" by a Lady Godiva procession.

Leofric died in 1057, and was buried with the Countess in the porch of the Church of the monastery they had founded. The lordship of Coventry then became vested in the Earls of Chester, afterwards passing into the hands of Henry III. and William d'Albany. In 1338 the manor of Cheylesmore, near Christ Church, was settled upon Edward the Black Prince, after the death of Queen Isabel, his mother. Under the Act redeeming the Land Tax, the Prince of Wales, afterwards George IV sold the manor to the Marquis of Hertford, who again sold it to Mr. H. W. Eaton, and he, on being raised to the peerage, took his title from the estate as Baron Cheylesmore.   The family still own the estate.

After Edward III granted the incorporation of the town in 1344, the city was encircled with walls three yards in thickness and

Peeping Tom

six yards in height, with thirty-two towers and twelve principal gates, the first stone being laid by the Mayor in 1355, but the progress of the work was not continuous, and it was not till forty years had elapsed that the wall was completed. It withstood all attacks for 300 years, enabling the inhabitants to bid defiance to the mandates both of Edward IV and Charles I, when those monarchs appeared before the gates with armed forces and demanded admittance. Shut Lane, a small lane off Far Gosford Street, leading to the Charter House district, marks the spot where the royal armies were refused admittance to the city, and history says that Charles II, piqued at his father being refused an entrance, ordered the destruction of the city walls in 1662.

In the year 1392, Richard II. made the administration of justice in the city distinct from the county by constituting a mayor, a recorder, and four of the chief inhabitants, justices of the peace. By a charter of Henry VI in 1451, "the County of the City of Coventry" was formed, and continued till after the passing of the Municipal Reform Act, 1835. During the Wars of the Roses, the gates of the city were closed against Edward IV, and he was compelled to retire; but after the battles of Tewkesbury and Barnet, he returned, and deprived the city of many of its privileges, which were afterwards restored on payment of a fine of 500 marks.

In 1842, Coventry was incorporated with the County of Warwick; in 1888 it was constituted a County Borough, and so it remains. Extensions of the boundary took place in 1890 and 1899, as already stated.

Three Spires

Having thus taken a cursory glance at the history and present position of Coventry we will start on our first walk. No visitor can fail to notice the beauty of the principal approach to the city. At the end of Eaton Road we are attracted by an ornamental ground a little over two acres in extent. Let us take a walk along the path towards the west, and pausing about halfway across enjoy a favourite view of the city, with the "three tall spires" pointing heavenward. This enclosure, Grey Friars' Green, so-called from the Grey Friars' Monastery, which once flourished close by, was formerly a part of the waste land of the Manor of Coventry, and was used as a common playground; it was also for a long time the chief site of the Annual Great Fair, which then lasted eight days, and is one of the eleven recreation grounds (large and small) which Coventry possesses, totalling to 97 acres. In this ground, at the narrow end, nearest the city, is a statue of Sir Thomas White, a native of Reading, whose benefactions to Coventry in the 16th century are largely enjoyed in the city. The statue was unveiled in October, 1883, by Mr. A. S. Tomson, then Mayor, whose good fortune it was on the same day also to declare open to the public for ever Spencer Park (the gift of Mr. David Spencer), and Swanswell Recreation Grounds (presented by Sir Thomas White's Trustees)—an occasion of much rejoicing throughout the city.

On the right-hand side of the main road are some modern and well-built villa residences, erected on leasehold land forming part of the Park Estate, belonging to Lord Cheylesmore. This Park was in olden times attached to the royal palace of Cheylesmore and, as before stated, was sold by the Prince of Wales to the Marquis of Hertford, by whom the demesne was enclosed. A portion is let in garden allotments, but a considerable and increasing area has in recent years been laid out for building purposes.

A little further, the Quadrant, a well-built series of residences, will be seen standing a little back from the road on the right. No. 10 is the home of the Y.M.C.A. and No. 2 is the headquarters of the District Nursing Institution, which is doing a beneficent work among the sick in the city. At the end of the Quadrant, fronting to Warwick Road, and also running some distance along Union Street, are the buildings of the Liberal Club, which, in addition to the usual clubhouse accommodation, has a spacious hall, much used as a place of public assembly. The handsome structure, which, with towers and domes stands nearly opposite, is the Warwick Road Congregational Church, erected in 1891 for the congregation of Vicar Lane Chapel, which dated back to 1723, the first minister being the Rev. Robert Simpson, grandfather of a vicar of St. Michael's bearing the same name. Imposing as is its exterior, the interior will be found quite in keeping, while in the rear are Sunday school and other rooms.

The neighbouring building with the flagstaff is the Reform Club, a well-appointed house of the Liberal party, opened by Lord Carlingford in 1883. Christ Church (to be hereafter noticed) stands to our right hand, and passing Bull Yard, the back entrance to the Barracks, on the left of the road, and Union Street and Warwick Lane on the right, we come into Hertford Street, where we have a full view of Holy Trinity Spire. Shortly, on the west-side we notice the handsome offices of Mr. Edgar Whittindale, a well-known auctioneer. The present edifice was erected in 1911, after a destructive fire, on the site of a stucco building with a castellated parapet. This was originally built for the use of a body of Dissenters : it afterwards became a Subscription Library, and being transferred to the Coventry Corporation in 1867, it was used as the first Free Public Library and Reading Room. Higher up on the same side of the street, with a useful projecting clock in front, are the offices of the Midland Daily Telegraph, Autocar, Cyclist, Photography, and other publications of the well-known house of Messrs. Iliffe & Son, Ltd. Here also is a branch of Parr's Bank.

On the right-hand side stands the Queen's Hotel, an elegant three-storied stone building, erected by a Company in 1879, which is

Reform Club

usually the home of the Liberal candidate at Parliamentary elections. The next building is the Coventry Savings Bank, which, previous to extensive reconstruction and alterations, was the Coventry Institute. The adjoining pile of buildings formerly belonged to Messrs. J. & J. Cash, textile manufacturers, but was purchased some years ago by the Government and converted into an up-to-date Central Post Office, of which the city had long stood in need. The wine and spirit stores of Messrs. Johnson & Mason stand next.

Almost directly opposite is the Empire Theatre, originally known as the Corn Exchange, which was a handsome structure of the Italian order, in red and white brick. The chief entrance was approached by a flight of steps surmounted by an open balcony ornamented with pillars. This building, which consisted of a corn exchange or concert hall, assembly room, etc., was erected at a cost of £7,000 by a Company formed in 1853, and was opened in 1856; but some years ago the Company disposed of the property to Mr. William Bennett, proprietor of the Opera House. The great hall was 110 feet by 52 feet, had a noble appearance, and would seat about 1,300 persons. In 1906 the building was converted into the present Theatre of Varieties, the memorial tablet of which was laid on 30th June by Miss Ellen Terry, the famous actress, who was born in Coventry. The handsome building next on the same side is the King's Head Hotel—a famous rendezvous—in a niche at the corner of which is the official effigy of Peeping Tom. And it may be remarked that this effigy is not a mere public-house sign.

The open space at the top of Hertford Street, where all tramlines meet, is called Broadgate; but leaving to the left, and Grey Friars' Lane to the right, we enter High Street (forming part of the London and Holyhead Road), when we see on our left one of the old houses for which Coventry is so noted. This house, at the corner of Pepper Lane, is a good specimen of the thalf-timbered houses which form one of the most interesting features of the

Pepper Lane

city.

Walking along High Street we pass on our right the Craven Arms Hotel, formerly a well-known old commercial and posting inn, and recently rebuilt in picturesque style; while next to it is the fine stone building of Lloyds Banking Co. On the left will be noticed the handsome building of Barclay & Co, Bankers, the front portion of which is utilised by Messrs. Gilbert & Son as a jewellers' shop. Proceeding, we leave Hay Lane on the left, and notice opposite thereto the London City and Midland Bank, Ltd, a really imposing block of buildings at the corner of Little Park Street. We now enter Earl Street, so named from having been part of the Earl of Chester's portion of the town. Immediately to the left is the new Council House, a magnificent pile, worthy of a great city. The foundation stone was laid, with much ceremony, on June 12th 1913 by Colonel Wyley, then Mayor. It comprises Council Chamber, Committee Rooms, accommodation for officials, etc, on a somewhat elaborate scale, but—no Town Hall, which is felt to be a deficiency.

The Old Palace Yard

If the visitor be not accompanied by a "guide, philosopher, and friend," he may at this point miss a "bit" of old Coventry worthy of more than a passing glance. Through the gateway there, to the left of the Herald Office, will be found the Old Palace Yard, so called on account of a building in which royal personages have been entertained.

Miss M. Dormer Harris, who has of late years written much on Coventry, notably a volume of Dent's Mediaeval Towns Series, in an illustrated article (Country Life Sept. 11th, 1915) says: "Palace Yard, anciently known as 'Mr. Hopkins's house in High Street,' has an unpretentious brick frontage with an entrance leading to a lovely gabled court adorned with lead work. Though the tradition, noted in an auctioneer's bill of 1831, that the house

The Old Palace Yard

contained the 'ancient palace and state rooms of Queen Elizabeth' is pure fiction, Sampson Hopkins did entertain an Elizabeth of Royal blood, and if the family already held Palace Yard in 1605, then it was here the Princess had her lodging—the Stuart Princess, not the Tudor Queen, but her namesake, who reigned for a winter in Bohemia, she to whom Sir Henry Wotton wrote the lines beginning: 'You meaner beauties of the night.' The other 'palatial' associations of the Hopkins's house gather round less romantic members of the House of Stuart—James II, his daughter Anne, and George of Denmark, Anne's husband, of whom Charles II said he had tried him drunk and tried him sober, and, drunk or sober, there was no making anything of him.

Though the quadrangle is a medley of styles—at the north end oriels, fifteenth century barge-boards, and gables of steep pitch, at the south a classic portico with Venetian window and bell turret—the whole is wonderfully harmonious." Time will not permit of an exhaustive examination. It may, however, be briefly quoted that to this "palace fallen on evil days," Princess Elizabeth was hurriedly brought in November, 1605, for safety within Coventry's walls, her tutor, Lord Harrington, of Combe, boding evil from the news of the baulked conspirators' wild ride through Warwickshire.

The chief remaining architectural glories consist in the artistic lead work: on an east side spout-head is inscribed the date 1655, on a western one 1656.

The accompanying letters H stand for Richard Hopkins and his wife Sarah (Jesson). Few to whom the place is familiar will disagree with Miss Harris's conclusion:— "Probably there exists no town house of this type and importance in England—save, may be, the New Inn, at Gloucester—better worth preservation; and yet the fear is always imminent that the site may fall a prey to the speculator, and the glories and memories of Palace Yard vanish.'

Leaving this interesting place, we cross over to St. Mary Street, where are the Police Buildings and modernised Justice Rooms, which were opened in September 1899, and cost the city upwards of £24,000.

The authorised strength of the police force is :—1 chief constable, 1 superintendent, 6 inspectors, 14 sergeants, and 115 constables — total, 137.

Leaving St. Mary Street, we have on our right the Technical Institute. The mean and narrow front gives no sort of indication of the extent and usefulness of this Institution. It was opened in 1887, the aim of the managers being to afford an organised system of technical education, in which both theoretical and practical instruction are so co-ordinated as to assist the trade and commerce of the city. Under happier circumstances a New Technical Institute would be nearing completion, plans having been passed two years ago for the erection on the Pool Meadow of a building in every way worthy of the cause. A little further, on the right, is an ancient residence, with overhanging- upper stories, and also the Old Star Inn, of some renown in former times. Opposite is Bayley Lane and with Much Park Street on our right, we enter Jordan Well, which received its name from Jordan Sheppy, once Mayor of Coventry, who sank a well here.

Further on, a number of old buildings are seen. Passing on the left Freeth Street and Cox Street (formerly called Mill Lane, on account of the Earl's mills once standing at the other end of it), and on the right hand White Friar Street, we reach Gosford Street, at the commencement of which will again be seen specimens of old houses, in good repair. Further along this street, on the right-hand side, is passed White Friars' Lane, which is entered by an ancient passage, while on the left is seen a brick-built chapel, with rooms for Sunday Schools at the rear, belonging to the General Baptists. The colossal building on the right hand side is a new engineering factory, erected partially on the site of a number of old houses at the front, and in the rear encroaching on the Workhouse Infirmary and grounds. In this particular locality are many timber-framed tenements—picturesque, but old. Shortly, the main street becomes wider, and then crosses the river Sherbourne. At this point there formerly stood a chapel dedicated to St. George, the patron saint of England, who, according to tradition, was born in Coventry (vide Percy's Reliques). St. George, who lived in the early part of the fourth century, is reckoned among the seven champions of Christendom, and the day set apart for him in the calendar of the church is the 23rd April. In 1474 Edward IV, then visiting Coventry, kept St. George's feast here, attending the chapel on this bridge for the service. Entering Far Gosford Street, we may find that a little further on the street crosses another bridge—called in former times Dover Bridge—now almost unnoticeable, although a copious stream of water at one time flowed beneath it, which was until recent years an important local boundary line. The space between the two bridges was called Dover — hence the name of the bridge.

On the right are the works of Messrs. Calcott Bros., Ltd., cycle and motor-car manufacturers, and the narrow passage next them, adjoining the stonemason's yard, is "Shut" Lane, where Edward IV and Charles I were shut out of the city. Edward IV tried to enter the city at Gosford Green and was refused admittance. To our left are other industrial premises. Lower Ford Street follows, and again on our right are All Saints' Schools, a brick building with stone dressings, containing accommodation for 347 children. Nearly opposite is an opening leading to Harnall Row, and a little higher up is All Saints' Church, of Gothic architecture, erected in 1868, the material used being the local red sand-stone.

Walking up the street, we pass on the left a number of old timbered houses, and also, near the end of the street, the Pitt's Head Inn, noted for the stabling of racehorses during the time that the Coventry races were held at Stoke, a short distance away. The stone-faced building further on to the left was formerly a cycle and motor works, but has recently been converted into shops, etc. At the top of the street is the fine triangular piece of common land called Gosford Green. It was on this plot of ground that the lists were appointed for the intended single combat between Henry Bolingbroke, Duke of Hereford (afterwards Henry IV), and Thomas Mowbray, Duke of Norfolk, in 1397. Richard II caused these two to meet at this place, he and a great array of his nobles being present. The Duke of Norfolk stayed the previous night at Caludon Castle, about two miles distant, while Hereford lodged at Baginton Castle, about the same distance away in another direction.

On the day named the two Dukes and their followers met, but when everything was in readiness for the fray the King stopped the proceedings, and banished Hereford for ten years and Norfolk for life. This remarkable scene is immortalised by Shakespeare in his play of "Richard II." It was on this Green also that Earl Rivers and his son were beheaded. Coombe Abbey, of some historical and antiquarian interest, and a seat of the Earls of Craven, lies about four miles up the Binley Road on the right, while Walsgrave Road on the left leads by the remains of Caludon Castle, to Wolvey and Leicester, the latter town being distant about twenty-four miles. Many new streets have recently been laid out in this vicinity, and the district is much favoured for residential purposes. A handsome church, dedicated to St. Margaret, has been erected on the Walsgrave Road; a little further on is Stoke Congregational Church; while yet further is Stoke Parish Church. Some distance to the right of Binley Road are the enormous cycle and motor car works of Humber, Limited.

Turning from the Green, we proceed along Payne's Lane, so called from a person who formerly owned the land. On the right we notice a large building surmounted by a figure of Britannia, this is the carpet and coach-lace manufactory of Messrs. Perkins & Co. A little further up on the left stand the extensive premises of the Sparkbrook Manufacturing Co.Ltd., while on the right will be noticed several streets leading to an entirely new district of well-built and convenient houses, adjoining which are the football grounds of the City Football Club, which plays under Association Rules.

We now turn to the left down East Street, in the lofty houses of which ribbon weaving was formerly carried on, the chief seat of that industry being the district of Hillfields, away on the right. Taking the first turn to the left, we find the South Street Council Schools, a fine set of buildings in red brick with stone dressings, well adapted for their purpose, and with accommodation for 1,156 children. These were one of the two blocks of buildings first built under the Education Act of 1870.

Proceeding down Read Street, on the left we pass the extensive cycle works of the Premier Cycle Co., Limited, and those of the Auto Machinery Co., Limited, where steel balls for machine gearings are made. In Hood Street, which we now cross, we notice to the left a large building, formerly occupied by Humber Limited, the well-known cycle manufacturers.   A great fire occurred here in July 1896, completely destroying the factory, of which the present one is the successor, and doing damage to the extent of £100,000.   It is now the works of the British Thompson Houston Co., used for the manufacture of electricity meters, etc. Proceeding into Alma Street, we find the Coventry works of the Dunlop Pneumatic Tyre Co., Ltd., occupying the site of what was at one time the Coventry Skating Rink, erected at the time when roller-skating was popular.

On the right are premises formerly in the occupation of Singer & Co., Limited (whose immense works are to-day in Canterbury Street, away to the right), and later occupied by several firms connected more or less with the staple trade.

Skidmore's Art Metal Works Co. were once located in Alma Street, one of whose productions was the beautiful screen erected in Hereford Cathedral, which was exhibited in the International Exhibition of 1862. Another production was the metal work of the Albert Memorial in London (the memorial to the Consort of the late Queen Victoria). In Raglan Street, close by, to the right, is the Roman Catholic Church of St. Mary, an edifice of brick with stone dressings, attached to the church being a convent, with a school which is conducted by the sisterhood.

Leaving" behind us Alma Street, we enter Lower Ford Street, with Lea & Francis' Cycle Works on our left. On our right is a fine brick building formerly used as a ribbon manufactory. The works have lately been modernised, and are now the splendidly equipped works and offices of the Coventry Plating and Presswork Company, Limited. In Perkins Street, adjoining, are the large works of Messrs. Wyleys, Ltd., wholesale manufacturing chemists. The modest building which comes next is the Rehoboth, or Calvinistic Baptist Chapel. Near by is the Parish Church of St. Peter's, constructed chiefly of red brick, the first stone of which was laid in 1840, its original accommodation being 1,254 sittings. The church was provided for a working class district, and it may be told in an whisper that its style of architecture has never excited the undue admiration of churchpeople. St. Peter's Schools, in Yardley Street, a few yards from the Church, have in their time done useful work. The present accommodation is for 468 scholars, but the building having been condemned by the Board of Education will be closed for public elementary school purposes, when circumstances permit.

At the corner of Cox Street is the Sydenham Palace Hotel, with the celebrated Stevengraph Works standing in close contiguity; and at an opposite corner has for some years stood the Alexandra Coffee Tavern, now undergoing transformation into a picture palace. Proceeding along Ford Street a fine view of the spires of St. Michael's and Trinity Churches is shortly obtained, while we pass on the left a roller-skating rink and the tobacco manufactory of Messrs. Banks & James, and on the right Wheatley Street Council Schools, opened in 1894, reckoned among the finest of their kind in the Midlands, and having accommodation for 1,112 children. At the back of these schools stand the large flour mills of Messrs. Robbins & Powers. A few steps further and we reach the Ford Street Primitive Methodist Church, opened in 1895, while opposite is a small edifice belonging to the Catholic Apostolic Church. The next place of interest is the Municipal School of Art on our left, an interesting building of brick and stone, erected in 1863, though the School itself was established in obscure rooms in the Burges in 1844. Over the front windows and door are semi-circular panels, in which are carved groups representing painting, sculpture,, architecture, mechanics, and pottery.

Next to these premises are the Holy Trinity Schools, built of local stone, and with their turret and spire much resembling a church in appearance, but now devoted to other purposes. There was formerly accommodation for about 1,000 children. Passing on, we reach Hales Street, when, turning to the left, we get a good view of the Market Hall tower and clock, while close at hand is the handsome and well-equipped Fire Station, opened in the autumn of 1902. The building stands on a portion of the Pool Meadow, a piece of land once covered with water, known as St. Osburg's Pool, and where the Coventry Great Fair is now annually, held for five -days at Whitsuntide. At the rear thereof is the public mortuary, opened in 1913. Nearly opposite is one of the only two remaining gates of Coventry, called Swanswell Gate, to which a portion of the city wall is attached. Adjoining the old gate is the Coventry Hippodrome, a handsome variety theatre.

Retracing our steps a few yards, we turn to the left up Jesson Street to the Stoney Stanton Road. On the right is St. Mark's Church, similar in design to All Saint's, and both of which were consecrated January 12th, 1869. The Schools connected with this church are some distance up the road, and have accommodation for 343. Adjoining the church are Swanswell Pool and Recreation Grounds, given to the city by Sir Thomas White's Trustees. The grounds were laid out and planted by the Corporation, and, as before stated, thrown open for the free use of the people.

By walking as far as the church, we may enjoy a pleasing view of the Coventry and Warwickshire Hospital. The original building, of the Victorian Gothic style of architecture, in the shape of a Maltese cross, contracted for at £5,162, was opened in 1866. To cope with the ever-increasing needs of the institution several important extensions have been made from time to time, the last additions being the Nurses' Home and the King Edward Memorial Wing. The Hospital is now complete and modern in every respect. The Hospital is a monument of voluntary effort, and the artizan classes contribute generously towards its support. The adjacent buildings are the several detached blocks of the City Hospital, a municipal undertaking where infectious diseases are treated under the superintendence of the Medical Officer of Health. The Corporation also has an Isolation Hospital for small-pox patients, which is situated at Pinley, in the rural district.

Returning to the space at the top of Jesson Street, on our right is a school for orphan daughters of freemen of Coventry. Leaving Leicester Street on the right (in which is the Girls' Industrial School and Home), we enter Cook Street, and pass under another ancient city gateway (lately purchased and presented to the city by Aid. W. F. Wyley) to the left of which the town wall may be traced to Swanswell Gate—the best remains of the wall now to be found. Cook Street contains many ancient houses. Chauntry Place, built on the orchard belonging to the old Priory, is passed on the left, and also St. Agnes' Lane, containing old buildings, and at one time a well, named after St. Agnes, to the waters of which were ascribed healing qualities. The "petrified kidneys" here illustrate the manner in which the whole of the city was

Cook's Gate

paved years ago. Near the wide part of the street once stood Cook Street College, the only remains of which are seen in some stone walls found in Rood Lane, on the right, where also will be seen above a doorway some curious stones with a defaced coat of arms.

Passing under a gateway, we enter Bishop Street - there are many ecclesiastically named thoroughfares in Coventry - and, turning to the right, we find at the top the terminus, offices, and wharves of the Coventry Canal Co. The Coventry Canal, constructed under Parliamentary powers obtained in 1768, is in length rather more than 32 miles, terminating at Fradley Heath, Staffordshire, a few miles north of Lichfield. By its junction with other canals it is an important medium of communication with London, Liverpool, Manchester, and other commercial towns and districts. The Coventry and Bedworth section was opened in August, 1769.

On our left hand is King Street, and on our right is the Foleshill Road, leading to Bedworth, Nuneaton, and Leicester. Adjacent to this road, lying a little to the left, on the opposite bank of the canal is a conspicuous building, originally erected by the Coventry Cotton Spinning & Weaving Company, to introduce a new industry to the city. In 1890 a serious fire took place, and owing to the trading of the company having almost continually resulted in a loss, business was not resumed. After a time it was re-built, enormous additions were afterwards made, and the whole of these immense premises are now occupied by the Daimler Motor Co. (1904) Ltd. About half-a-mile beyond this, and on the right-hand side of the road, is Bird Grove, the house in which the celebrated novelist, "George Eliot," resided with her father, her birthplace being about six miles further on. The house and grounds are now in the hands of the speculative builder, and will soon be entirely obliterated. Streets of artizans' dwellings now stand on this historic site. The municipal Electric Light Works and Refuse Destructor stand near the canal on the

George Eliot

Charles Bray

left of the road. A little further distant are the factories of Messrs. J. & J. Cash, Ltd., textile manufacturers, and then the handsome works of Messrs. Courtaulds, manufacturers of artificial silk and silk goods. A tram-car ride for a couple of miles along this road is full of interest.

The line of Bishop Street is continued by St. Nicholas Street, taking its name from a church long ago standing on this, the most ancient site of the town. At the other end of St. Nicholas Street is situated "Rose Hill," where "George Eliot" spent much time with Mr. and Mrs. Charles Bray, both well-known for their literary and philosophic work. The ground here is very elevated and is called Barr's Hill, "Barr" being, it is said, an old Gaelic or Welsh word for summit. Corley Rock, an escarpment of interest to the geologist, but very much "weathered," is about four miles away, and less distant in this direction also, at the summit of an eminence, are situated the Corporation reservoirs, which were brought into use in 1895. The water stored there is pumped from borings at Whitley, about three miles distant across the city, and a supply of pure water is thence distributed by gravitation. Coventry now derives an auxiliary supply of water from the Shustoke Reservoirs, by agreement with the Birmingham Corporation. Owing to the tremendous growth of the population serious measures will now have to be taken to further augment the water supply.

Returning down Bishop Street an exceptionally picturesque view of a portion of the city lies before us. Through a gateway on the right we shall find some curious old buildings. On the left we pass the end of Silver Street, connecting with Cook Street, where once stood a stone cross of some historical renown. It was known as Swine's Cross, and was removed in 1763 to widen the street. The fine old-fashioned building standing next is used as a Mission Rooms connected with Holy Trinity Church, but was previously known as St. John's Hospital, and formerly an old parsonage house stood at the back. The Coventry Grammar

School for many generations had its home here, and among its more famous scholars was the celebrated historian, Sir William Dugdale, who was a schoolboy here from his tenth to his fifteenth year (1615-1620). Facing this building is Well Street, and to the left runs Hales Street, in which, on the left hand side, stands the Royal Opera House, which is about to be rebuilt on ambitious lines; further on is an extensive agricultural implement warehouse, and a little beyond on the opposite side is the City Smithfield, where there was once a collection of water from the Sherbourne, now arched over.

Retracing our steps a little and turning to the left we enter the thoroughfare known as the Burges—not Burgess, if you please, as the name is derived from the bridges through which the Sherbourne flows in this neighbourhood. On the left hand is the covered way into Palmer (or Pilgrim) Lane, a thoroughfare apparently as ancient as its name, wherein are situated the works of Messrs. Caldicott and Feltham, the printers and publishers of this Guide. The opening by the right there, at the side of the premises of Messrs. Comley and Son, house furnishers, although officially designated 'Court 3,' is generally known as the Lancasterian Yard, from the fact that an undenominational day school, the forerunner of the "British" School, was opened there in 1811, on the system founded by Mr. Joseph Lancaster. We now enter Cross Cheaping, and a few steps bring us to a quaint old building, with wooden rails in front, occupied as leather warehouses.

Passing Ironmonger Row on the left, we notice on the right a shop of fine construction, occupied by Messrs. Mat-terson, Huxley and Watson, Limited, ironmongers, etc., whose extensive foundry and warehouses lie at the back. Between the doorways of the two next shops will be found a curious carved oak statue of St. George killing the dragon.

Moving past West Orchard on the right, with the Little Butcher Row opposite, many venerable timbered houses on each side deserve notice. This has been an animated and busy part of the town from the time that the market was held around the Cross, from which the street derived its name. The original Coventry Cross was set up in 1423, and taken down in 1510. Another cross was completed in 1544. It was six-sided, each side being seven feet wide at the base, and it was 57 feet high, with 18 niches. The canopy was beautifully adorned with statues, one of which, representing Henry VI., now stands in the kitchen of St. Mary's Hall. The pillars, pinnacles, and arches were enriched with a variety of figures and flags, on which were displayed the arms of England, or the rose of Lancaster; and there were likewise representations of the trades of the city. On the summit was a figure of Justice, and the work was finely finished throughout. In 1669 the Cross was thoroughly repaired, and so highly decorated that it became the admiration of the time. From this date, however, it appears to have been neglected and allowed to decay, and in 1771 the remains were wholly removed.

On our left is an opening into the Great Butcher Row, with Trinity Church close by, though unfortunately hidden by the buildings in front. Opposite is the Market Place, at one of the corners being the premises of the Coventry Coffee Tavern Company, Limited, now called the Central Cafe, standing on the site of the old Mayor's Parlour, or Justice Room, which was erected in the year 1584. One of the shops under the tavern buildings is occupied as the office of the London and North-Western Railway Co.   The open space a little further on is the Wholesale Market, while the proximity of the Market Hall is indicated by the clock tower, the Fish Market being separated from the main hall by an arcade.

Returning, we come into Broadgate, on the left-hand side of which, near the top, is the office of the Coventry Standardly the oldest local newspaper, established in 1741. The thoroughfare takes its name from a gate which stood on the left at the

Little Butcher Row

end of Grey Friars' Lane, leading to the old Manor House at Cheylesmore. This gate was the advanced part of Cheylesmore Castle, as described in the Earl of Chester's Charter in the time of Henry II. The old Broadgate was an ancient street, and as narrow as Grey Friars' Lane, of which, in reality, it was a continuation towards the Cross. The present broad street was made in 1820, by pulling down a number of old houses. Previous to the erection of the Market Hall, the general market for the city was held here. Here also the hustings were erected when public nominations at election times were in this particular neighbourhood, as many present inhabitants can testify. And here will finish our first perambulation, which it is to be hoped proved richly interesting.

For our second walk, we will start from the King's Head Hotel, at the corner of Smithford Street. As we look down this important business thoroughfare we cannot but notice what a picturesque effect the old houses, with their projecting gables, and the fine embattled tower of St. John's Church in the distance, give to the view: it is one of the best street views in "ye ancient citie."

The first house on our right is the City Hotel, which formerly had a verandah, from which many an exciting scene, especially during election times, was witnessed. It has, however, been re-modelled and re-decorated as an hotel and restaurant. Immediately adjoining is a succession of old houses, the fronts of which show a good proportion of timber work, though some have been filled up with brick and other materials in such a way as to destroy their former quaint appearance. Passing on, we come to a narrow passage on the left, called Vicar Lane, where a building known for many years as the Vicar Lane Congregational Chapel is occupied by the British Photo Engraving Co. The first meeting house of the Society of Friends was in this lane, a much more ancient building than Vicar Lane Chapel.

Market Hall.—Returning down the lane we cross over into Market Street, which leads to the Market Hall, with its lofty clock tower. The building is erected partly on the site of the old butter market and watch-house, near which formerly stood the city stocks. The materials used are brick and stone, and the cost of erection was about £20,000. The building consists of one large hall, 140 feet by 93 feet, with four entrances; a smaller hall, partly let as shops, and an arcade. The tower is 135 feet high, and contains a fine clock, with illuminated dials, the cost of which was £300. The hall was opened in 1867 with an Art and Industrial Exhibition. In Market Street, by the way, was born the celebrated actress, Miss Ellen Terry, and two houses have put forth claims for the distinction of being the birthplace.

St John's Church

Retracing our steps into Smithford Street, the next place to be noticed is the old Theatre Yard on the left. The Theatre was erected by Sir Skears Rew, a member of the Coventry Corporation (who then resided in the building in front) and opened for public performances on Easter Monday 1819, but was superseded on the opening of the Royal Opera House in Hales Street.

On the right is Drinkwater Arcade, named after a popular mayor, and adjoining is the new Corn Exchange, erected on the site of the old Post Office. Just below, on the left, we come to the Barracks, with stone buildings facing the street, entered by a gateway. The Barracks were erected on the site of the once famous Bull Inn, within whose walls many a stirring event took place. Here the hapless Mary Queen of Scots was confined as a prisoner. The rooms fronting the street are the officers' quarters, next to these being offices and the quarters of the married soldiers. Under the second archway is the stabling, over which are the rooms occupied by the rank and file. Then there is a spacious drill-yard, which was formerly a bowling green connected with the Bull Inn. Facing the visitor as he enters the drill-yard is the hospital, while to the right and left stand the riding school, guard-room, canteen, workshops, etc. The outer gate of this yard opens into the Bull Yard, a short thoroughfare which emerges at the bottom of Hertford Street.

Returning to the main entrance, and passing a short distance down Smithford Street, we notice on the right a large red brick building. This is the Great Meeting House, now belonging to the Unitarians. It was erected in 1701, partly on the site of an ancient structure called St. Nicholas' Hall, or Leather Hall, and is fitted up in old-fashioned style, with oak pews and galleries. In connection with this place of worship is Smith's Charity, yielding about £100 per year, which is at the disposal of trustees.

A little further down the street, on the right, we come to the central stores of the Coventry Perseverance Co-operative

Society. A bridge, known as Ram Bridge, not visible however, is now crossed, and passing by the end of West Orchard, on the right, Fleet Street is entered, marking the site of the ancient fleet, or overflow of the Sherbourne, which passes under the bridge. Fleet Street got its name for the same reason as Fleet Street, London.

St. John's Church — We now leave the main street, and, turning to the right, enter Hill Street, passing the east end of St. John Baptist Church. This edifice, which was restored in 1875, is a noble specimen of mediaeval church architecture. Its-origin is traceable to the religious guilds of the city, and Queen Isabel, by a grant dated May 7th, 1344, gave a piece of land at Bablake whereon to erect a chapel, which was dedicated in 1350. This chapel was very small, only occupying the space now taken up by the chancel. In 1357 a former valet of Queen Isabel took an interest in the fortunes of this chapel, and by his gifts facilitated the work of extension; he also endowed the place to such an extent that four additional priests could be maintained. Two years afterwards other lands were given by Edward the Black Prince, and buildings appropriate to a collegiate institution were added. On the suppression of religious houses the church and its property were granted to the Mayor and Corporation of Coventry, but services were not regularly kept up. During the time of the Commonwealth the church was used as a temporary prison, and many Scotch soldiers were confined in it. It was repaired in 1734, and service has since then continued to be held. The interior is one of the most beautiful, as well as most peculiar, in the Midland Counties. On the last day of 1900 the church was much damaged by a great flood, the water rising to a height of nearly six feet. Since then further renovations have been carried out, and a new organ provided.

Bablake - Adjoining the churchyard of St. John's stands a venerable building, in an excellent state of preservation, founded as a school in 1560 by Thomas Wheatley, mayor. It is called Bablake

School, a name derived from a water conduit once near this place. The building is not now used as a school, but as parochial rooms in connection with St. John's Church, the Charity Commissioners having by a new scheme united several of the charity boys' schools, and permitted the erection of a fine building in Coundon Road. The number of scholars in the old school was seventy, who remained two years, half the boys during the second year living indoors. Their uniform was a long tunic of blue cloth with yellow linings, black trousers, a heavy knitted worsted cap, with a yellow tuft. The interior of this ancient building is of no small interest to the archaeologist. In 1832 an additional schoolroom, with master's residence, was erected on the west side of the spacious playground, but this was demolished in 1897 to make room for the offices of the General Charities Trustees. These trustees are now the managers of the new school.

Bond's Hospital Adjoining is Bond's Hospital, a rare example of half-timbered work, with old-fashioned gables and windows. The hospital was founded by Thomas Bond, a draper in Coventry, in 1506, "for the reception of ten poor men, and a woman to dish their meat and drink." By his will he directed that they should have "every year a gown of black with a hood, and that they be every day at the beginning of matins, mass, and evensong," and also that the said ten men should "daily, after they had supped, go into the church, and there, kneeling, every man to say fifteen paternosters and fifteen aves and three creeds in the worship of the passion of Christ, and then to drink and go to bed." The hospital is very conveniently arranged, and the rooms are airy and pleasant. Each inmate has a portion of ground for cultivation. The charity provides for forty-five old men, each of whom receives 6s. per week, and eleven of them reside in the building, in separate rooms, the accommodation being for eighteen. The present building was erected 1832-3 on the site of the old hospital.

Quitting this interesting institution, and leaving Bond Street

— which is built on the old Town Wall — on the right, we ascend Hill Street. The high brick walls on the left enclose two burial grounds—one belonging to the Society of Friends, and the other connected with West Orchard Chapel. Interments here being very rare, it may be mentioned that the late Miss Mary Ann Cash was buried in the Quaker Ground so recently as the 15th of April, 1916. Miss Cash was a member of an old Coventry family, known for her good works, and had reached the exceptional age of 97. In a humble building adjoining the West Orchard Chapel Ground, bearing the inscription on the front -Sunday Schools 1779 - the first Sunday Schools opened in Coventry were held. Opposite are the works of the Leigh Mills Co., where many work-people are employed in the manufacture of woollen goods of high quality.

St. Osburg's Church — Bangor Street is now passed on the left, and Gas Street on the right, and further on to the left is found a fine building comprising the schools, with teachers' residences, belonging to the adjacent Roman Catholic Church, dedicated to St. Osburg. The church stands on the site of a chapel first built here in 1807. The present Gothic structure, the peculiar material used in the construction of which will be noticed, was consecrated on September 9th, 1845, the funds having been raised by the Rev. Dr. Ullathorne, who then held the priesthood, and was afterwards consecrated Bishop in the Church that was due to his pious zeal. The spire was subsequently added. The dimensions of the interior are 151 feet by 50 feet, and the decorations, especially those of the Lady Chapel, are very rich. Services are performed by members of the Order of St. Benedict, who reside in the brick-built Priory next to the church.

Reaching the top of Hill Street, we have in front of us Coundon Road, leading to the railway station of that name, on the Nuneaton and Leicester branch. Near to the station are the schools (opened in 1890) of the Bablake foundation scheme, in which Bablake, Fairfax's, Katherine Bayley's, and Baker, Billing and Crow's Charity Schools are now amalgamated. The front elevation of the building is 244 feet in length, and is in the Elizabethan style of architecture, possessing a central tower and oriel window over the front entrance. The building is in red brick with stone dressings, and the schoolrooms and workshops are fitted up in the most approved style. Barras Lane runs to our left, while to our right is Abbott's Lane. Going down the latter, we pass the site of Naul's Mill, or Hill Mill, a very ancient mill, which gives name to Naul's Mill Park, close by, and the rear of the old Gas Works on the right, and Mill Street and Stephen Street are to the left.

Old Gas Works.—Turning to the right into Gas Street, we find there the main entrance to the Old Gas Works. The first works for supplying Coventry with gas were erected by a number of private gentlemen in 1821, but in 1856 an Act of Parliament was obtained under which a public company was formed, with 800 shares of £25 each. Great improvements and additions were from time to time made at the works, which were kept in a very efficient condition, and the financial result to the shareholders was satisfactory. In 1884, however, owing to advances being made by the Corporation, an arrangement was made by which it was agreed that the whole undertaking should be transferred to the local authorities. The amount of the purchase money was £168,000. As before remarked, new works have been constructed at Foleshill, and the old buildings are now used mainly for storage purposes.

Going to the end of the street, we cross Hill Street, bearing a little to the left, and pass through Bangor Street to the Holyhead Road, running out of which is Dover Street, containing St. John's Schools, with accommodation for primary education for 538.

Turning down the road, passing on the left a meeting house and school belonging to the Society of Friends, and a Chapel of the Plymouth Brethren, we enter Spon Street, facing Queen Victoria

Road, having to our immediate left hand the main entrance to St. John's Church. Moving to the right, we traverse Spon Street, a name supposed to be derived from the "span" between two fords of the Sherbourne, one being originally at the bottom of Smithford Street, where, as we shall presently see, a bridge is built.

Houses of more or less antiquity are in plenty along this street, while on the left is the great watch and engineering factory of Messrs. Rotherham & Sons, a firm known in all parts of the world. A few steps onward bring us to the offices and show rooms of Messrs. Rudge-Whitworth, Ltd, whose factory occupies a large part of Crow Lane and Trafalgar Street close by. To cope with their enormously increasing business, this firm have erected an immense steel girder building at the rear of their offices, and extending from Spon Street to the river Sherbourne. Proceeding still along Spon Street, we pass on the left a covered way into Meadow Street. More old houses appear, and on our right is Barras Lane, with the Jews' Synagogue a short distance up. Also on our right, standing back from the line of houses, is St. Saviour's Mission Church, connected with St. John's Church. Sherbourne Street, to the left, is reached, and opposite is a brick building, at one time the meeting place of the Mormons, but subsequently used as a Mission Room. In close proximity are the Spon Street Council Schools. These are an admirable cluster of buildings, and include departments for boys, girls, and infants, to the number of 1,205.

Water Works — A narrow lane at the far end of these schools leads to the Spon End works of the City Water Department, whence for many years the greater part of Coventry's water supply came. According to an ancient document, the inhabitants, in 1334, obtained from Edward III a license to erect in Well Street a conduit twenty feet long and ten feet broad. As the population increased, wells were from time to time sunk in various parts of the town, and, previous to the establishment of the Spon End works, there were in existence more than thirty public pumps, most of which have since been removed. The works we are now viewing were constructed from plans prepared by Mr. Hawkesley, C.E., and consist of filtering beds and a pumping station, the original outlay being about £20,000. Owing to the continued increase of population, additions have been made at various times to the capacity of the works, and, as previously stated, the Corporation felt the necessity of establishing an additional pumping- station at Whitley. The combined supply is good, both in quality and quantity, but as a safeguard, the Corporation, a few years ago, contracted for a further supply from the Birmingham reservoirs at Shustoke, a wise precaution, as this auxiliary supply is now generously drawn upon.

Leper House — Returning to the street, we find a very old stone building, sometimes called the Leper House or Hospital, now divided into tenements. The formation of the place can be best seen by looking at the side facing the gardens. Dugdale says this "Chappel or Hospital of Sponne" was founded by Hugh Keveliok, Earl of Chester, in the time of Richard III, the Earl having a certain knight of his household who was a leper, and endowing it for the maintenance of such persons as were afflicted in like manner in the City of Coventry. A priest (with brethren and sisters) was located here, together with the lepers, "praying to God for their benefactors." The hospital afterwards belonged to the Crown, but in the reign of Edward IV it passed to the canons of Studley, Warwickshire, on condition of their praying for the King and others. Some antiquaries think this was not the place for lepers, but that a building in Chapel Fields was devoted to their use.

Crossing the bridge over the Sherbourne, we can take a look at the ornamental grounds of the Water Works, and then pass into Spon End, viewing its old houses. The viaduct in front is connected with the Coventry and Nuneaton Railway. There are twenty-two arches, which were originally built of stone, but in 1857 many of them fell with a tremendous crash, happily without causing loss of life, and they were rebuilt of blue brick. Close to the viaduct, on the left, standing back a little from the line of the street, is St. Thomas's Mission Church.

On a house at the corner of Melbourne Road, to the left, there is a quaint proclamation against vagrancy. Beyond is Chapel Fields, a large outlying district on the Old Allesley Road, formerly inhabited largely by watchmakers, with schools in Lord Street connected with Queen's Road Baptist Church. Hearsall Common, a considerable piece of open land, used as a recreation ground, adjoins the district on the south and south-west side.

Reversing our walk a little, and bearing to the right, we enter the Butts, which in former times was set apart for the practice of archery; there were also two others, Summerland Butts and Barker's Butts. The pleasant-looking building there on the north side is Sherbourne House West, the Y.W.C.A. Hostel and Institute, opened June 3rd, 1915. Passing Hope Street on the left, we come to Albany Road, a fine thoroughfare on the right leading to Earlsdon, a populous and growing suburb situated pleasantly on high ground, where watchmaking was once extensively carried on ; the cycle and motor trades are now also represented. To the right is the entrance to the grounds of the Coventry Cricket Ground Co, where "most do congregate" the lovers of athletic sports. The grounds are fourteen acres in extent. Opposite is St. Thomas's Church, Vicarage, and Schools, standing on a piece of land purchased of the freemen. The church is of native stone, and of simple design.

Continuing along the Butts, we find Thomas Street on our left, and a little further on to the right, in Upper York Street, are the grounds of the Coventry Public Cattle Sales Company. Here also are the great mechanical engineering and machine tool works of Messrs. Alfred Herbert, Limited. York Street turns off to our left. A well-known hostelry, at the sign of the "Hen and Chickens," brings us to the eastern end of the Butts, Hertford Place turning off to the left. We are now entering Queen's Road, which extends from this point to the Warwick Road end of Stoneleigh Terrace. Queens Road Baptist Church stands to the right, and, with its pinnacled tower, presents a somewhat imposing appearance. It belongs to the Baptist congregation which for a long period worshipped in Cow Lane Chapel, and the origin of which dates back over 200 years. This edifice, in which there are sittings for about 1,000 persons, was formally opened on the 1st May, 1884. The style of architecture is perpendicular Gothic. The interior is well arranged, and the whole effect is one of neatness and comfort. Classrooms were afterwards added, the total cost approaching £ 12,000. In 1912 considerable additions were built at the rear, comprising a handsome hall for general meet-ings, concerts and the like, together with a smaller lecture hall and other apartments.

In the centre of Queen's Grove, just past the chapel, we may see an oak tree planted in commemoration of the Sunday School Centenary in 1880. Here also is a memorial in honour of the late Mr. James Starley, to whose genius the origin, develop-ment, and perfection of the modern bicycle and tricycle are greatly due. The St. John's Cycle Works, formerly carried on by his sons, were in Queen Victoria Road, on our left, but are now, with suitable additions, used as the headquarters and drill hall of the local Territorial Battalion. Grosvenor Road, on our right, is the most direct road to Spencer Park, presented to the city by the late Mr. David Spencer, of Coventry, and, as before stated, publicly opened in 1883. The park comprises eleven acres, and cost about £7,000. The park is divided by a thoroughfare which forms part of Spencer Avenue, and the portion south thereof has recently been laid out at considerable expense in tennis courts and bowling greens, and a handsome pavilion erected.

Christ Church and the Grey Friars — Returning to Queen's Road, and passing on, with the handsome residences of Stoneleigh Terrace on our right and Grey Friars' Green on our left, we reach

Warwick Road, and, turning to the left,, make our way to Christ Church, standing on the site of the old Grey Friars' Monastery, to which the spire originally belonged. For 300 years after the removal of the monastery this spire stood alone. The Grey Friars sprang from St. Francis, an Italian; they lived wholly on charity, and, with wallets on their shoulders, generally went about in couples collecting alms. Their monastery here was one of the last to fall into the hands of Henry VIII, who compelled the friars to sign and seal their own surrender. The site and remains were given to the city in 1542. The buildings must have been of very considerable extent, for the present church stands easily within the space formerly occupied by the nave of its predecessor. The land afterwards passed into private hands,, the Corporation retaining the spire. In 1823 a movement was set on foot to build a church, the spire and 150 guineas being granted by the city. The church was opened in 1832. The entrance consists of a finely-arched doorway, with smaller ones on either side. The interior is very plain; the nave measures 101 feet, and there is room for about 1,500 persons, 900 of the sittings being free. Christ Church was formerly a chapel-of-ease to St. Michael's, but in March 1900, it was granted a separate and independent parish, taken out of St. Michael's,

Going along Union Street, we find on our left the recently erected parochial buildings connected with Christ Church. Taking the first turn to the right, we are speedily on the site of the grounds and ancient Manor House of Cheylesmore. Here, says Dugdale, the Earls of Chester, to whose lineage Leofric belonged, "had an eminent seat, bearing the name of a castle in those olden times." Some remains of the place will still be found after passing under the ancient gateway. The buildings on the eastern side are in many parts raised upon stone walls of great strength. The works of the Swift Cycle Co, Limited, are near this spot, and opposite to them are the offices and works of Messrs. Hobart Bird & Co., Limited, another firm of cycle and motor cycle manufacturers.

Retracing our steps to Union Street, we go along Cow Lane, to the right, and find up a covered passage Cow Lane Chapel, built in 1793 to hold about 700 people. The old chapel has been entirely altered, and a lecture room and useful class-rooms constructed, where a great religious and social work is carried on by the authorities of Queen's Road Baptist Church, including men and women's Adult Schools, Sunday Schools, girls' classes, men's club, etc.

"Black Gift" — On the other side was Baker, Billing, and Crow's Charity School, which was merged into the Bablake School in 1887. This school was founded by Mr. Samuel Baker, of London, in 1690, and the charity further augmented by various benefactors.

A little further along, on the same side, are the extensive works of Messrs. Thomas Bushill & Sons, printers and manufacturing stationers.

Ford's Hospital — Returning, we move to the right into Grey Friars' Lane, where we find a most interesting relic of old Coventry. Grey Friars' Hospital, or Ford's Hospital, was founded by William Pisford, a merchant of Coventry, under his wall dated 1509. It was originally intended for aged couples "of good name and fame." The charity now provides for thirty-seven aged women, eleven of whom are in residence at the hospital in separate rooms. The structure is a model of old timber work, and is considered one of the most beautiful specimens of its kind; John Carter, the antiquary, quaintly saying, "it deserves to be kept in a glass case.

Warwick Lane is to our left, in which are the Wesleyan Methodist Chapel and Sunday Schools. The chapel was opened in 1836, and will hold about 900 persons. .Some years ago it was re-seated and renovated, and a school and class rooms built by its side. It has recently been again renovated and still further improved.

The fact is well authenticated that John Wesley preached in Coventry on several occasions. The lane in which we now stand owes its name to the fact that before the opening of Hertford Street it was the way of the city to Warwick, through which the coaches had to pass. Coming back past the hospital, we notice the old houses adjoining, and, passing the Standard printing office on our right, presently emerge into High Street, and here end our second "walk."

I

Starting from Broadgate, we pass along High Street, and turn into Little Park Street, leading to that part of the Cheylesmore estate formerly comprising the Little Park. Directly on our right is a building now occupied as the Club House of the Manchester Unity of Odd Fellows, where visiting brethren are gladly welcomed. The business of the different lodges is here transacted, and the recreation of the members provided for. A few steps further and we reach the handsome new block of buildings comprising a hall and other offices for the Masonic fraternity. There are four Lodges of Free and Accepted Masons in Coventry — Trinity, Stoneleigh, St. Michael's, and St. John's: the first-named being a centenary lodge (dating from 1785). On the same side of the street, also, is a fine old red brick house containing the County Court and District Registry Offices.

Passing Cow Lane on the right, we find ancient houses on each side. Up Court 2 will be seen some old buildings forming a square, with carved doors, beams, etc. Close by, on the same side, stands one of the best of the restored old houses in Coventry, now forming part of Messrs. Middlemore's bicycle saddlery works. It was in former times . occupied by Mrs. Katherine Bayley. A school was established in accordance with a will made by Katherine Bayley, and was opened in 1733 in a building adjoining the Draper's Hall, at that time eight boys and eight girls being admitted.

From the year 1742 a sermon, followed by a collection, was annually preached at St. Michael's Church on behalf of this school. In 1868 the number of boys was 52, and was eventually increased to 54. The last uniform of the scholars consisted of dark cord trousers, drab waistcoat and coat with blue facings, and cloth cap. The charity was managed by ten trustees, and Thomas Sharp, the Coventry antiquary, held office for many years. The school is now amalgamated with the Bablake Foundation in Coundon

Road.

Along the street old buildings are still met with, and at this point once stood a fine old mansion built by Simon Norton, in 1610, a chimney-piece belonging to which is now in the dining-room at the old Bablake School. Some build-ings on the left, bearing a raised cross, will be noticed, and these are joined at the back with other ancient buildings. The front part of the house next to that bearing the Cross was once used as a Roman Catholic Chapel. We now reach St. John's Street, for some time called Dead Lane, generally supposed to be so called owing to the plague of 1478, when 3,000 people died in the city. Dead Lane, however, was known as Dede Lane two centuries before the plague. (Le Dedelone, date 1300, Miss Mary Dormer Harris). The tradition is a popular and picturesque error. At the corner of St. John's Street, Little Park Street and Park Side, a building used to be devoted to the purposes now served on a much larger scale by the Coventry and Warwickshire Hospital, Stoney Stanton Road. It afterwards became the Warwickshire Reformatory School for girls. The City Council, however, purchased the prop-erty for public improvements, the school having been removed by the county authorities, and the site has been re-occupied by dwelling houses. Nearly opposite are the imposing buildings of the Swift Motor Co, Ltd, the Maudslay Motor Co, Ltd, and the Siddeley-Deasy Motor Car Co, Ltd, motor works.

The amenities of this neighbourhood are much depreciated by industrial necessities. Owing to the local authority's lack of powers to compel reasonable building lines and the setting back at necessary points traffic here is very dangerous.

Beyond the end of Little Park Street is Coventry Park, of which in the time of Edward III one Thomas de Quinton was appointed keeper of the pasturage on payment of £5 annually "and reserving sufficient grass for the deer." About 1388, a piece of land was separated from the main part, the one being called the Little Park and the other the Great Park. Beautiful avenues of trees formerly adorned the park, which was opened to the people as a place of recreation till the time of its enclosure by the Marquis of Hertford. Very little of the original sylvan character of the park is now to be discerned. In addition to the works mentioned a large number of modern dwellings have been erected, and along Quinton Road a barracks for the Howitzer Brigade, R.F.A.

Near this spot, in a place called the Park Hollow, in 1510, Joan Ward and seven others were burned for heresy, as in 1521 was Robert Selkby, and in 1553 Laurence Saunders suffered in like manner. In September, 1910, in honour of these Coventry martyrs, a memorial was unveiled in the presence of a large number of citizens; it will be found occupying a commanding position in Quinton Road, and to be well worthy of inspection.

The Memorial is in the shape of an old-style Celtic cross, in silver grey Cornish granite, which with the steps of the pedestal reaches to a height of twenty feet. On the side towards Coventry is a laurel wreath, and below the arms of the city, both designs being worked in gun metal. On the opposite (the south) side is the inscription :—

This memorial was erected by public subscription in the year 1910.

On the west side is the following :—

Near this spot eleven persons, whose names are subjoined, suffered death for conscience sake, in the reigns of King Henry VIII and Queen Mary, namely: In 1510, Joan Ward. On April 4th,

1519, Mistress Landsdail (or Smith) ; Thomas Landsdail, hosier; Master Hawkins, skinner; Master Wrigsham, glover; Master Hockett, shoemaker; Master Bond, shoemaker. In January, 1521, Robert Selkeb (or Silksby). Also, on February 8th, 1555, Laurence Saunders. On September 20th, 1555, Robert Glover and Cornelius Bongey.

On the east side :—

It is recorded that the Martyrs were burned in the Little Park, "the same place where the Lollards suffered." The Martyrs' Field (now built upon) was situated 200 yards from this spot in an easterly direction.

The last words spoken by Laurence Saunders were:—

"Welcome, the Cross of Christ! Welcome, everlasting life."

The new buildings over there at the corner of Mile Lane are further evidences of Coventry's industrial expansion; while a little higher up the same lane are other works, and also the Cheylesmore Council Schools, with accommodation for 1,254 children.

Retracing our steps a little and turning to the right we find ourselves in Park Side. Here on the left are some remains of the old city walls. The thoroughfare on the same side is a short street actually named "Short," and containing some municipal dwellings built on the small Hat system. Continuing along Park Side we presently reach Paradise Street, which descends to a point opposite the Workhouse, or "London Road Institution."

Coventry Cemetery — Turning to the right we approach the pretty entrance to the Coventry Cemetery, and if there is a feeling of pleasure at the outside appearance of this "hallowed ground" that feeling is enhanced when we make a closer acquaintance with what is reputed to be one of the most beautiful burial places in the kingdom. The cemetery comprises eighteen acres of land, the natural features of which were favourable for the purpose, and were fully taken advantage of by the late Sir Joseph Paxton, under whose direction the work was designed and carried out. The "ample gravel walks," says one who writes upon the subject, "winding in all directions, and revealing at every turn some new beauty to the eye, attest the artistic skill of the plan; and the long broad promenade next the turnpike road commands a most charming view." There are two chapels, and many monuments, the one near the entrance (to Sir Joseph Paxton, who for some time represented Coventry in Parliament), claiming special attention. A portion of land at the south-east corner is assigned to the Hebrew community. The Cemetery was opened in 1847, and the cost of it was more than £12,000. The London and Northwestern Railway runs along the south side, and beyond is Whitley Common, a large portion of which was, in 1887, added to the Cemetery, being connected therewith by a bridge over the railway. The total area is over 30 acres.

Leaving the Cemetery, and turning to the right a short distance down the London Road, on the left we find an avenue of trees, at the other end of which is the Charter House, the site of an old Carthusian Monastery. The order was founded by one Bruno, of the Monastery of Chartreuse, of which word "Charterhouse" is a corruption. The life led by the monks was of most exclusive and hermit-like character. A large part of the boundary wall is still standing at the back of the present buildings, and in the garden are traces of some of the ruins. About a mile further along the main road stands Whitley Abbey, and the ruins of the fire-destroyed Baginton Hall are some three miles distant.

White Friars' Monastery — Making our way back towards the city, the "three tall spires" come in sight, and at one point we find that Holy Trinity spire is obscured by that of St. Michael's, the first effect of this eclipse being rather bewildering.

Leaving Paradise Street to the left, with Gulson Road to the right, we reach the Workhouse, the buildings in connection with which are on the site of, and indeed some of them actually formed part of, the ancient Monastery of the White Friars, who appeared in Coventry about 1343, and who claimed the prophet Elias as their founder. Their house was built by Sir John Poultney, Lord Mayor of London, and was enlarged by a gift of land from William Bottener in 1413. The annual income of the monastery in the time of Henry VII dwindled down to £7 13s. 8d, and the monks were turned out without pension or allowance of any kind. The place afterwards passed to several owners, among whom was John Hales, who in 1565 entertained Queen Elizabeth there. Mr. Hales here originated the Grammar School. After his death, the house passed to other hands more than once, and in 1801 it was sold to the Directors of the Poor of the city, who at once adapted it to the requirements of a workhouse. There are still many interesting remains of the Monastery to be seen here, notably the cloister, now the dining-room of the inmates; but in the alterations which have necessarily been made there is a large mixture of the modern with the ancient. There were formerly two workhouses — one for Trinity Parish in Well Street, and one for St. Michael's Parish in Hill Street. The present establishment has room for about 500 inmates. A large infirmary was in 1890 added to the main buildings, but there have since been important extensions.

Continuing our perambulation we notice a modernised public-house, "Ye Olde Salutation Inn," the first within the boundary on this side of Coventry, and having a pictorial sign with the legend "You are welcome to the city." A few steps further on there is a stone against the front wall of a house, the inscription on which is hardly legible : — "90 miles from London."

Leaving White Friar Street on the right, we enter Much Park Street, which has been supposed to derive its name from being the way to the Great Park already mentioned, but it was well-known in former days as "Misford Street," and the etymology is doubtful. Immediately to the left hand are St Michael's Schools, stone built, and having for the purposes of elementary education accommodation for 546 children. Old-fashioned houses abound hereabouts, and a little way down the street, on the right, is an old gateway, which was connected with the White Friars' Monastery, and now leads into White Friars' Lane, in which is St. Mary's Mission Church, attached to St. Michael's. Nearly opposite this will be noticed with pleasure a fine old building of timber and plaster, part of which is devoted to the purposes of a brewery. Some good old houses are passed on the right, then we cross Earl Street, and, bearing a little to the left, enter Bayley Lane.

St. Michael's Church now appears, which in passing along we shall have on our right, while we notice some of the buildings in the neighbourhood. Immediately to our left is the Hall of the Drapers' Company, built in 1832, in the Grecian style. The chief feature of the interior is the ball room, measuring sixty feet by thirty feet. The lane was formerly monopolised by drapers' shops. St. Mary Street follows, on the right-hand side of which stand the new Police Offices, previously noticed.

St Mary's Hall

St. Mary's Hall

A few steps further bring us to that fine mediaeval relic, St. Mary's Hall, one of the chief glories of the city. Erected in the time of Henry VI for the guilds of St. John, the Trinity, and St. Katherine, the building affords striking evidence of the wealth and importance of those bodies, though there were many other guilds connected with the trades of the city. On passing through the doorway, the curious carving on the roof of the porch will be noticed; it is said to represent the Deity crowning the Virgin Mary, and the Annunciation. On the right of the courtyard are some massive vaults, with groined roof and arches, containing some interesting relics.

Crossing the yard, we enter a lobby with doorways leading to all parts of the building. Turning up the noble staircase, passing by a fine tapestry, we enter the Great Hall, a noble room, 76 feet long, 30 feet broad, and 34 feet high. This was the banqueting hall of the guilds, whose entertainments were on a princely scale, and which monarchs and nobles did not refuse to honour by their presence. The timber-work of the roof contains figures of angels with musical instruments. The grand window at the end of the hall is divided into nine compartments, filled with stained-glass figures of several of our kings, with their coats of arms, each placed under a canopy. Originally, the work of putting in this window was executed by one John Thornton, a native of this city, who also put in the east window of York Minster.

Under the window, and extending along the whole breadth of the hall, with a depth of ten feet, is the celebrated piece of old tapestry. This exquisite work is divided into six compartments, formed into two rows of three each, one above the other. The figure representing Justice in the centre of the upper square occupies the place where there was originally a representation of the Deity, which for some reason was cut away. A few years ago the tapestry was restored, and afterwards exhibited for a time at South Kensington.

At the other end of the hall is the Minstrel Gallery, approached by a narrow staircase, and behind is a large room called the Armoury. In front of the gallery hang some specimens of the ancient civic armour, which are brought into requisition for the "city guard" that generally marches at the head of the Godiva procession.

On the west side of the hall is the oriel, containing a figure of Godiva, and sometimes the chair of state, of carved oak, bearing the City Arms (Elephant and Castle). This chair has often been the seat of royalty. There are some good paintings on the walls, and the windows are of modern stained glass, with the names of some of the mayors of the city. The Mayoress's Parlour is found up the steps opposite the oriel, and in it are many interesting pictures and antiquities. Returning through the Great Hall, under the gallery we have a look into the old Council Chamber on the right.

Another room on the left formerly contained the splendid collection of muniments of the city, but these are now preserved, in a building (specially erected for the purpose) adjoining St. Mary's Hall. Of these documents a writer has said—"Few, if any, of the corporate towns of the kingdom are possessed of such a vast collection of muniments, so historically precious, so genealogically valuable, so locally interesting. Adopted, as the city was, by one of the most influential of Saxon thanes, cherished amongst the most powerful Norman barons, basking in the sunshine of royal favour during the reigns of succeeding sovereigns; in its monastic institutions, the abode of learning; in the houses of its merchant princes, the home of riches — it is not to be wondered at that during the lapse of more than eight centuries so many literary treasures should have been accumulated."

A cursory examination will show that this eulogy is not undeserved, and that the Corporation have acted wisely in providing a separate building for the storage and preservation of this priceless collection. In 1895, Mr. John Cordy Jeaffreson, B.A., one of the Inspectors of Ancient Writings for Her Majesty's Commissioners of Historical Manuscripts, prepared a "Calendar" of these "Books, Charters, Letters Patent, Deeds, Rolls, Writs, and other Writings," and stated that "the number of MSS. in the Muniment Room that still are, or were some fifty or sixty years since (i.e., prior to part of them being bound up in volumes) separate writings, may on a cautious and moderate computation, be said to exceed 1,000."

Under the Minstrel Gallery are some steps which lead into the kitchen, where there is evidence of the scale on which preparations were wont to be made for civic feasts. "What is that curious effigy on the buttress, there ?" it may be asked. Ah! that nearly life-sized figure is a painful reminder of less civilized days. Read the inscription on the brass plate :—

This Knaves Post

was formerly affixed to the wall of a house in Much Park Street. It was usual to sentence offenders to be whipped at the cart tail from the Mayor's Parlour (in the Market Place) to the Knaves' Post and back.

The post was erected in this place

AS A RELIC OF THE PAST,

By order of the Corporation, May, 1900.

Leaving the Hall we turn to the left, and on the west wall of it we find a similar reminder of more barbarous times in the City Stocks, which were used as lately as the boyhood's days of some living citizens. The inscription reads :—

THESE STOCKS

formerly stood in the Market Place (where they were used for the punishment of offenders) until the year 1865.

They were erected in this place

AS A RELIC OF THE PAST,

By order of the Corporation, May, 1900.

A favourite subject for artists comes next in the shape of a fine old-timbered house, which is maintained in perfect condition; and immediately following is St. Michael's Baptist Chapel, built in 1858, for about 600 people. In 1898 the authorities of the chapel provided a new organ, by Nicholson & Lord, of Walsall, which is one of the most satisfactory in the city. A Sunday School is held in a room under the chapel.

Hay Lane runs to our left, and Bayley Lane continues in front, with many old houses and the County Police Office. Turning here to the right, we have on our left the recently enlarged County Hall, formerly the Assize Court. Here are now held Quarter Sessions and weekly Petty Sessions for part of the county, also monthly sittings of the County Court. This building, with the gaol which once stood at its side, was erected in 1785, and belonged to the Corporation, but in 1842 it was transferred to the county, at the price of some £17,000. The assizes being removed to Warwick, the gaol was rendered useless, and Mr. Alderman Gulson purchased the site, presenting it to the city for the purpose of erecting thereon a building for the Free Public Library, that for some time had been carried on in the premises in Hertford

Street of the old Coventry Library, the 17,000 volumes of which were transferred to the city on advantageous terms.

Free Library — The late Mr. Samuel Carter at once gave £1,000 towards the new building, and Mr. Gulson then handsomely undertook the completion of the work, which cost more than £4,000. The internal fittings cost about £2,000, contributed by citizens. The erection was carried out by Mr. J. Marriott, Coventry, from designs by Mr. E. Burgess, of London, and the building was opened in 1873. The reading-room is commodious and well lighted and arranged. Tuesday, July 8th, 1890, saw the completion of another generous gift to the town, by Mr. John Gulson — a new Reference Library. The room is 66 feet long and 53 feet broad and is built of red brick, with Ancester stone dressings. Inside, above the corridor or alcoves on the ground floor, runs a gallery, which as below, is occupied by books. The walls are partly covered with encaustic tiles, and the floor is of pitch pine blocks. The Library is a well conducted Institution, and borrowers are allowed free access to the books.

Mr. Gulson spent upwards of £11,000 on the buildings, which form a noble memorial of both his generosity and foresight. Mr. Carter's contribution was devoted to internal fittings. The Committee of the Coventry Industrial and Fine Art Exhibition with which the Market Hall was opened in 1867 had a final balance of £775, which they donated to the purchase of books (vide brass plate inscription in the entrance lobby of the Reference Department). On the death of Mr. Gulson in 1904, the Library was further enriched by his collection of books and etchings, together with a sum of £500. A fine portrait of the deceased gentleman adorns the wall at the west end of the Reference Library, and special book cases and furniture constitute his memorial; his memory is held in the greatest reverence by all citizens.

At the east end of the Reference Library is a large painting by

Luca Giordano, entitled "Bacchus and Ariadne," presented to the city by the late Right Hon. Edward Ellice, who for a long period represented Coventry in Parliament. It formerly hung above the Minstrel Gallery in St. Mary's Hall. Several other pictures are exhibited, and there is also a fine collection of water-colours.

It should be mentioned, however, that all the work of the Library Committee is not now carried on at the central institution. In 1910, the Council accepted an offer from Mr. Andrew Carnegie to provide new Libraries at Foleshill, Stoke, and Earlsdon, at a cost of £10,000. Sites were obtained and buildings erected, each comprising a news and reading room with reference books, a lending department, and a juvenile department. All three were officially opened on the same day, 20th October, 1913, by the Mayor (Col. Wyley).

On June 4th, 1914, Mr. Carnegie was the City's guest. He expressed himself as delighted with the libraries, and he remarked that America had nothing to teach Coventry in planning, constructing, and equipping such buildings. As part of the day's function Mr. Carnegie was presented with the honorary freedom of the city.

According to the last published report, on March 31st, 1915, the stock of books in the libraries numbered 77,721 volumes, and the total number of issues during the year ending at the same date was 350,591. The number of books issued in the Reference Library was 43,409, and this in addition to constant use of works on the "open shelves," of which, of course, no record can be made.

We now walk along the road between the Library and Holy Trinity Church, a spot where once stood an old building called Jesus Hall, taken down in 1744. At the end of the road we have the main entrance to Holy Trinity Church. Opposite this is Derby

Lane, which still exhibits some of the characteristics of Coventry's ancient thoroughfares.

Trinity Church, it is thought, was built some time before St. Michael's, the date at which it is first mentioned being 1269. It is of Gothic architecture, and the steeple is 232 feet in height, rising from the centre of the church, and supported on four massive pillars. The original spire was blown down in 1664, causing much damage to the body of the church. The east window, erected in memory of Mr. B. S. Cox, a parishioner, is a beautiful work of art. The church is in the shape of a cross, and consists of chancel, nave, and north and south aisles.

The aspect of the interior is as pleasing as the effect of the exterior is bold and striking. In 1855-6 the church underwent a thorough repair and restoration, the galleries being taken down, the ceiling illuminated with blue and gold, and some fine windows introduced. At the same time the tower was opened and the bells removed from the lantern, the whole structure being, it was thought, endangered by their ringing. During the progress of the work a curious fresco painting was discovered in the space above the springing of the west arch that supports the tower. This picture, which is now invisible, was a representation of the "Last Judgment," and as far as could then be made out the centre figure was that of our Saviour in a crimson robe, seated on a rainbow, with the earth for a footstool. Below were the Virgin Mary, St. John, and the Twelve Apostles. Two angels were sounding the summons to judgment, and the tombs were giving up their dead.

On the right was a flight of steps leading to a portico, over which angels were looking down on the dread scene. Others were giving welcome to a figure wearing a tiara, evidently intended to represent a Pope, who, having passed by St. Peter, was the first to enter heaven. On the left of the Judge were unhappy spirits being dragged to the place of torment. Another fresco was found near the north vestry door, but that too, has faded away.

There are but few monuments in this church, and perhaps the only one to call for note is the tablet on the south wall of the choir to the memory of Dr. Philemon Holland, who was a physician and a schoolmaster, and prided himself on having written a folio volume with one pen—an old one when he began, and not worn out when he had finished. The pulpit is of stone, and is handsomely carved. The font is very old, and is painted and gilded. The finely-sculptured reredos in Caen stone was erected to the memory of Mr. John Bill, the father of the late Mr. John Bill, the work representing the visit of the Magi, the Crucifixion, and the Ascension. The vestry contains a portrait of the late Dr. Hook, Dean of Chichester, who was for some time vicar of this parish. The organ has been re-built and enlarged at a very heavy cost, and is now a magnificent instrument.

Butcher Row - Leaving the church, we find ourselves in a small square formerly called the Spicerstoke, or Grocers' quarter, and then come to the Butcher Row, with a cluster of old houses on our left, and Broadgate appearing through the opening in front. We turn to the right, still in the Butcher Row, which, as its name denotes, was formerly the quarter in which the meat trade specially flourished. The butchers had houses on each side of the row, the upper parts being used as the dwelling places, and the lower as slaughterhouses and shops. A short distance down on the left is the Little Butcher Row, with a quaint bit of architecture at the far end, where the overhanging storeys nearly touch the next building. The wider part of the street below the row is known as the Bull Ring. The Spotted Dog public-house now stands on the site of the west entrance to the old cathedral.

Retracing our steps for a short distance, we turn to the left and enter Priory Row, passing more old houses, some of them being in a very good state of preservation. Next to these we find the Girls' Blue Coat School, built upon a portion of the site of the ancient Benedictine Monastery and Cathedral. The school presents a handsome appearance, and harmonises well with its surroundings. The charity was founded in 1714 by voluntary subscriptions, for the purpose of educating and training poor girls. The income of the school is about £300 a year, derived from bequests and other sources, including a collection after an annual sermon at Holy Trinity Church. A recent scheme has somewhat modified its ancient character.

Coventry Cathedral — In 1856, during the re-building of the school, the interesting remains we now admire were laid bare. The neighbourhood is of interest to the antiquary, for here once stood the convent from which the city is said to have taken its name, and which, according to Dugdale, was founded by "the Holy Virgin St. Osburg, and destroyed in 1016 by Canutus, King of Denmark, and that infamous traitor, Edricus, who, invading Mercia with an army, burned and wasted many towns in Warwickshire."

On the ruins of the convent, in the time of Edward the Confessor, Earl Leofric and his Countess, Godiva, founded a Monastery for the Benedictines, who derived their name from St. Benedict. The Monastery, with its Cathedral and Bishop's Palace, comprised a splendid collection of buildings, extending from the lower.part of the Butcher Row down to Priory Street.

The remains before us are those of the west front of the Priory Church, which was one of the Cathedrals of the united Diocese of Coventry and Lichfield until the Reformation. In the 12th century the Prior of the Cathedral held the position of a mitred Abbot, with a seat in Parliament as a spiritual Peer. Robert de Limsey was appointed to the custody of the Monastery in the reign of

Priory Row

William Rufus, and removed his seat from Chester to Coventry, thus becoming the first resident Bishop of Coventry. He seems, however, to have had little regard either for the building or the monks, for it is recorded that "besides his scraping much silver from a beam, he suffered the buildings to decay for want of repair; plundered the church of many ornaments ; and as for the monks he kept them to poor and miserable commons; neither regarding their regular living or anything that might advance learning among them; to the end that being thus brought low and in ignorance their thoughts should not soar so high as to consider the redress of these, his great injuries." The Bishop's Palace stood at the north-east corner of St. Michael's Churchyard. The Cathedral is supposed to have been in construction similar to that now standing at Lichfield (Lichfield Cathedral is older than that at Coventry : Coventry Cathedral is supposed to have been a copy of it), and to have occupied a site on a gentle declivity from the north side of Trinity and St. Michael's Churches down towards the Sherbourne.

Within the walls of this Monastery many historical events took place. In 1404 Henry VI. held a Parliament in the great chamber at the priory, at which no lawyer was allowed to be present: hence it was called Parliamentum Indoctorum, and sometimes the Laymen's Parliament. In 1411 the Prince of Wales (afterwards Henry V) was arrested here by John Horneby, then mayor of the city. In 1453 the place was visited by King Henry and Queen Margaret, who slept within its walls. Parliament again met here in 1459, and this time was called Parliamentum Diabolicum, on account of the number of attainders passed against Richard Duke of York and his followers; but these proceeding's were set aside the next year at Westminster. In 1510 Henry VIII. and his Queen came to witness the pageants of the city, and afterwards stayed at the priory. Two days were spent within its walls by the Princess Mary, who came to see the Mercers' pageant in 1525. The Monastery, of course, shared the fate that the Reformation brought upon all similar institutions, and all now left of the magnificent structure are these ruins and other fragments that we shall meet with.

Proceeding along Priory Row, we have on our left a burial ground belonging to Holy Trinity Church, whose bells, eight in number, hang in the curious wooden erection now seen. On our right are Trinity and St. Michael's Churches, of both of which we have fine views. Passing by Hill Top we see some handsome houses, and under one of them we find the offices and stores of a spirit merchant. There is here a fine range of vaults, extending under the ground some distance, and forming a remarkable portion of the Monastery remains.

Going down to Priory Street on the left, we see another burial ground which is connected with St. Michael's Church, in which is a memorial to Thomas Sharp, author of several works on the History and Antiquities of Coventry, who died 1841, aged 70 years. His memory is also perpetuated by a stained-glass window in the Mercers' Chapel, St. Michael's Church. A short distance down the street, on either side, are the extensive works of the Triumph Cycle Co, and a little further, on the right-hand side, are the Public Baths. These were opened in 1894, and cost (exclusive of land, which was already the property of the Corporation), £20,361 3s. 1d. Alterations and additions were made in 1905 and 1907. There are a gentleman's first class swimming bath, 90ft by 35ft, gentlemen's second-class swimming bath, 90ft by 35ft, a ladies' swimming bath, 60ft by 35ft, and 53 "slipper" or private baths. The want of further accommodation is now being keenly felt in the summer months. During the winter months the gentlemen's first class swimming bath is used as a public assembly hall. There is a branch establishment at Primrose Hill, opened in May, 1913, containing 35 private or "slipper" baths.

Turning to the right, we cross into New Street, supposed to have derived its name from some tenements put up to accommodate the workmen employed in building St. Michael's Church. Old houses are to be seen even in "New" Street, and also in Cox Street, which runs at the bottom. In Grove Street, found by crossing Cox Street, is a building, formerly, a chapel belonging to the Primitive Methodists, but now used as a printing office. Returning to the top of New Street, to our left stands the Coventry Provident Dispensary, a building worthy of the name and objects of the institution. The older part of the building was the original Dispensary, which was established in 1831; but such has been its progress that considerable additions have been made. The members, of whom there are some thousands, subscribe one penny per week, which entitles them to medical advice and medicine when required. The Institution is registered under the Acts relating to Friendly Societies, and is of great service to the community.

Taking now a look at the restored east end of St. Michael's Church, the noble edifice on which our eyes have often rested as we passed around it, we move along the beautiful avenue of lime trees which extends the whole length of the churchyard, and presently reach one of the chief entrances to the edifice, the survey of the interior of which will not disappoint the highest anticipations of the beholder. For its size as a parish church, St. Michael's claims first place in the United Kingdom. The earliest mention of the church is in the time of King Stephen, about the middle of the 12th century, when it was given by Ranulph, Earl of Chester, to the Monks of Coventry. The tower and steeple were afterwards added. The tower was built at the cost of two brothers, who for twenty-two years expended annually £100 on the work, commencing in 1373 and finishing in 1394. Their names were William and Adam Botener, citizens and many times mayors of Coventry. To their two. sisters, Ann and Mary, the erection of the spire is due, as is also the middle aisle of the church. An old brass plate once in the church declared that

"William and Adam built the Tower, Ann and Mary built the Spire; William and Adam built the Church, Ann and Mary built the Quire."

The tower rises immediately from the ground at the west end to a height of 130 feet 8 inches. It is enriched with well proportioned windows, carved figures, and tracery work of fine character. Upon this tower stands an octagon, 32 feet 6 inches high, supported by flying buttresses, and from within the battlements of this octagon springs the graceful spire, rising to the total height of 295 feet. This perfectly-proportioned and graceful structure never fails to win the admiration of those who behold it, and it is naturally an object in which the inhabitants of the city take great pride.

The church itself is 293 feet 9 inches in length, and 127 feet in breadth, and consists of nave, chancel, two aisles equal in length to the nave, and two smaller aisles. The church is intersected by massive pillars, supporting the arches of the roof, and the scene, from whatever point of view, is most impressive. In 1849 the galleries were removed and the pews made low and open, and in 1851 the church was first lighted with gas, now superseded by electricity. The windows are a beautiful feature, many of them being filled with stained and painted glass, some of it very old. There is a fine window to the memory of Albert Prince Consort, and the names of others are honoured in like manner.

The church was at one time divided into a number of chapels, with separate altars. The monuments are not very numerous, but several will be found worthy of notice.

One is a brass with the portrait of a woman kneeling, temp. James I, with the following lines engraved :—

"Her zealous care to serve her God,

Her constant love to husband deare,

Her harmless harte to everie one,

Doth live although her corps lye here.

God graunte us all, while glass doth run,

To live in Christ as she hath doone."

"Ann Sewell, ye wife of William Sewell, of this cytty, vintner, departed this life ye 20th of December, 1609, of the

age of 46 years. An humble follower of her Saviour Christ, and a worthy stirrer up of others to all holy virtues."

The most noteworthy brass in the church, however, is fixed on the wall near the south porch. It is called Scrope's Brass. Of the time of Queen Anne, it bears the following inscription :—

"Here lies the body of Captain Gervase Scrope, of the family of Scropes, of Bolton, in the County of York, who departed this life 20th of August, Anno Dui 1705, aged 66.

"An epitaph written by himself in the agony and dolorous pains of the gout and died soon after."

> "Here lyes an old toss'd Tennis Ball;
> Was racketted from spring to fall,
> With so much heat and so much hast,
> Time's arm for shame grew tyr'd at last.
> Four kings in camps he truly served,
> And from his loyalty ne'er swerv'd,

Father ruin'd and son slighted,
And from the Crown ne'er requited.
Loss of estate, relations, blood,
Was too well known but did no good ;
With long campaigns and pains oth' gout
He cou'd no longer hold it out,
Always a restless life he led,
Never at quiet till quite dead,
He marry'd, in his later days,
One who exceeds the common praise;
But wanting breath still to make known
Her true affection and his own,
Death kindly came, all wants supplied
By giving rest—which life deny'd."

Connected with the church is a splendid peal of ten bells, cast in 1774, and a clock with a chiming apparatus. There was a peal of bells here as early as the year 1429.

Tuesday, April 22nd, 1890, brought to a successful issue one of the most important works of parish church restoration ever undertaken in this country, for tower and spire, and much of the church, including the east end, which had never before been finished, were restored at a total cost of nearly £38,000. The whole structure is now one of great beauty and magnificence. The Archbishop of Canterbury, Dr. Benson, preached the re-opening sermon. The organ is a very fine one, by Willis, of London.

Leaving the church, we complete the walk up the avenue, and standing near the Free Library can obtain a view of ecclesiastical architecture that is well nigh unique. Then, turning to the left, we walk between the two churchyards and enter Hill Top, a curiously steep and narrow cobbled thoroughfare passing over the site of the Priory.

We now come into New Buildings — a name arising from some houses built here to make room for people whose homes outside the city had been destroyed in anticipation of a siege, in the time of Charles II. Passing on and turning to the left, we find old houses on the right, and on the other side a large brick factory and house, at first built for the manufacture of ribbons, but, by the generosity of the late Mr. John Gulson, for many years used as the drill rooms and armoury of the Coventry Rifle Volunteers, now merged in the local Territorial Battalion. The premises have also for many years been used by the Coventry Ragged Schools, which, notwithstanding modern progress, appear still to be a necessary, as they are a useful, institution. Entering the yard by the gateway, we see the Stevens Memorial Hall, a most useful recent addition to the Ragged School premises. Further remains of the Cathedral are also seen, with the Girls' Blue Coat School built upon them.

We now go past the Bull Ring, on the left, into Ironmonger Row, and at once come to a corner building on the right-hand, which, until a comparatively recent date was a public-house called the " Pilgrims' Rest." The windows, the cornice of the roof, and the porch of this house are worthy of attention, the materials of which they are constructed having been portions of an ancient building for pilgrims that once stood here, in connection with the Priory, the gatehouse of which was near at hand. On a stone inserted in the building are the words: "Upon this site stood the western part of a large and very ancient edifice called the Pilgrims' Rest. It was supposed to have been the hostel or inn for the maintenance and entertainment of the Palmers and other visitors to the Priory of Benedictine Monks which stood near, to the eastward. It became ruinous, and was taken down.

Next comes Palmer Lane, being the way the Palmers came from St. John's Hospital to the Priory. We can see that this lane is a very old part of the city, but the houses have lost their distinctive features. If we go up court 3, however, we shall find a building bearing evidences of age and importance. There is a fine old staircase, with the remains of an opening for a lift and a pulley. The beams of the rooms are of oak and very massive, while the sides are wainscotted with oak also. The place is now let as tenements. Further down the lane we see old timbered houses with projecting storeys, and then make our way through the passage into the Burges, and turning to the right go on to Well Street, which contains many old houses, on the right being some with gables of black and white. In Chapel Street, on the right-hand side, is Well Street Congregational Church, built in 1827, providing seats for 800 persons. It is a brick building, with stucco front, the entrances being under a portico. Several alterations and improvements have from time to time been carried out, the most important being in the year 1888, when it was found necessary to provide larger accommodation, both in chapel and schools. At a cost of £1,500 the chapel was considerably enlarged and the schools entirely rebuilt on a greater scale. Further considerable additions were made in 1898, a new Lecture Hall and Class Rooms being erected on land presented by Mr. J. T. Moy, a deacon of the church, and in 1905 a new building was erected at the side of the main edifice to provide for Young Women's Classes.

Coming down to Well Street again we see in front the cycle factory of Messrs. Clark, Cluley & Co., while next are some old timbered houses. Down a yard between two of these are a number of houses showing the old style of construction very plainly. One of these was in 1883 struck on two different occasions by lightning, and the end taken away. The Workhouse for Trinity Parish stood at one time nearly opposite this spot.

Passing on, more old houses appear, one with a gable facing the street having the vine carved on the ends; another shows, well the framework, and the cornice to the roof is carved with a Vandyke open pattern; still another shows a remarkable old style of building. Leaving Bond Street to the left, we go along

Upper Well Street, and come to a junction of several streets called Hill Cross, with Lamb Street on the right. On the opposite side is Cherry Street, with a chapel of the Plymouth Brethren. Leaving this and turning to the left we move into King Street, named after a person who owned land here. On the left we find the carpet and coach trimming manufactory of Messrs. Dalton & Barton, and then comes the British School, erected to carry on the institution started in the Lancasterian Yard, and previously noticed. This school was disbanded some time ago, and a girls' school took its place, thirty-six of the girls being for two years clothed and educated from a charity founded in 1731 by two ladies named Bridget Southern and Frances Craner. Since 1911, however, it has been used as a school clinic, under the Education Department.

We now make our way down Upper Well Street and enter Bond Street. Turning to the left into Hill Street, and passing through Fleet Street we enter West Orchard, where once was an orchard belonging to the old Priory. On our right are the extensive premises of the Coventry Perseverance Co-operative Society, including a useful Assembly Hall. Herein is conducted by the Society a large and successful Evening Continuation School. A little further along, on the left, standing back from the street, is West Orchard Congregational Chapel, succeeding a former edifice, erected in 1777, and afterwards on several occasions enlarged. It was formerly hidden by buildings in front. In 1820 the old chapel was taken down, and the present fine building erected, and at the same time some houses in front were cleared away. In 1856 the frontage was renewed, and the interior rear-ranged and modernised, with seats for 1,000 persons. New rooms built at the right front of the chapel, have an effect that is scarcely pleasing to the eye, the chapel being hidden from view on that side.

In this ancient thoroughfare a number of old houses with wooden frames and of various heights and descriptions are to be seen on the right, followed by the Market Hall. We now emerge into Cross Cheaping, a short distance from where we started on this, not the least memorable of our walks through the ancient city.

IV

We will begin our fourth portion of the perambulation of the city with a railway ride. Taking train for Foleshill, on the Nuneaton branch line — opened in 1848 — we travel for about a couple of miles along the west and north-west side of the city, obtaining a variety of interesting views of ancient and modern Coventry that are to be had in no other way. At Foleshill we notice that the enterprise of the residents has led to a not inconsiderable extension of station accommodation. Starting for a walk through some of the outlying districts within the area of the municipality, we leave the station on the side whereat we alight. Let us turn to the north-west along Holbrooks Lane for a short distance. First of all we are bound to notice the immense engineering establishment of Messrs. White and Poppe, Ltd. Then there is Foleshill Park, a recreation ground of a little over 23 acres, purchased in 1914. On the opposite side is St. Paul's Cemetery, which was transferred from the St. Paul's (Foleshill) Burial Board on the extension of the city in 1899. Additional land since purchased has brought the total area to a little over eighteen acres. Returning, and crossing the railway into Lockhurst Lane, we shortly notice a comfortable and commodious club house for the local Liberal party. Still on the left hand is the substantial and modern woollen manufactory of Messrs. Poole, Lorrimer & Tabberer. On the right is the Wesleyan Chapel, with newly-erected Sunday School buildings at the rear; and then again on the left more engineering- works of Messrs. White & Poppe, Limited, the Livingstone Mills of Messrs. W. H. Grant & Co, silk manufacturers, and the mill of Messrs. Pridmore & Co, manufacturers of elastic webbing, etc.

Emerging on to the Foleshill Road — part of the main road from Coventry to Leicester, via Nuneaton — we perceive adjacent to Broad Street, nearly opposite, St. Paul's Church and Schools, of the architectural character of which probably no one feels very vain. Proceeding along the main road, outward bound, we notice several more important industrial concerns, and a handsome hotel, "The General Wolfe," which has taken the place of an old-fashioned roadside inn. Then we reach Edgewick Council Schools, with accommodation for 600, and further along the road Foleshill Road Independent Church and Schools, the former being a building of the severely plain, old-fashioned type. Down the lane at the side we find another block of Council Schools, Little Heath Schools, with accommodation for 273, and a little distance away, on the banks of the canal, the iron foundry of Messrs. Alfred Herbert, Ltd., and also a manufactory of artificial stone. Retracing our course somewhat, and crossing by Edgewick Schools to Stoney Stanton Road — another main road from Coventry into Leicestershire — we find ourselves at Paradise. The general aspect of the district is not in harmony with notions suggested by the euphonious name of Paradise, but the neighbourhood is one to which the natives are said to be very much attached. There is no episcopal church just hereabouts, but there are a couple of chapels belonging to the Wesleyan and Primitive Methodist bodies respectively. There are also a couple of co-operative stores, and, on the Coventry side of the canal bridge, the generating station of the Coventry Electric Tramways. On the outward side of the same bridge are the works originally erected by the Cycle Manufacturers' Tube Co., which were purchased by Messrs. Mulliner & Wigley, Ltd, and were later acquired by Messrs. Charles Cammell & Co Ltd, of Sheffield. The concern has now developed into the Coventry Ordnance Works, Limited.

The industrial and residential growth of this portion of Coventry has been most remarkable, and there is, fortunately, every prospect of its continuance. The nearly-new Council Schools, with accommodation for 1,202 children, testify to the growth of the population hereabouts. Passing along Red Lane we reach the breezy common land known as Stoke Heath, and by crossing it and turning to the right, where the aspect is truly rural, we may reach the Barras Green district, or Upper Stoke, and passing by a block of Council Schools, with accommodation for 1,216, emerge on another main road leading to Leicestershire, in fact, direct to the capital of that county, via Wolvey. In this direction Coventry has extended very rapidly in recent years, a great number of new streets having been laid out. On the hill to our right we may notice Stoke Congregational Church, and the newly-built Church of St. Margaret, but turning to the left along the road we reach the ancient and interesting parish church of Stoke, with its vernal graveyard. Retracing our steps a little, and turning to the left, we may cross through Stoke Park, a pleasant estate of small villa residences, and reach yet another road to Leicestershire, via Binley, Coombe, Brinklow, to Lutterworth, with beautiful woodland scenery all the way. The spacious greensward opposite is known as Stoke Green; flanked by villa residences, and having a ground marked off for the use of a cricket club of more than local celebrity. We may here board a tram car and return via Gosford Green to Broadgate, being afforded frequent glimpses of the industrial and other aspects of this side of the city, and signs of its expansion in various directions.

It is, of course, impossible to exhaust our subject in the limits of a handbook. Apart from descriptions of its recent industrial and social condition, the history of Coventry, on an adequate scale and proper method, would fill volumes. In these obiter dicta much, very much, has perforce been omitted. Before taking leave of our visitor, however, we may perhaps briefly mention a few additional facts of interest.

The arms of the City are an Elephant and Castle, surmounted by a Cat. The legend is Camera Principis, or "The Chamber of the Prince." This is an indication of the Royal favour which Coventry has at various times enjoyed.

In 1436 Henry VI. visited Coventry, and kept Christmas at Kenilworth. In 1450 he attended St. Michael's Church, heard mass sung, and presented to the church a golden altar-cloth. In 1465 Edward IV and his Queen visited Coventry.

Prince Edward visited the city in 1474, and was presented with a cup and £100. In 1477 the Prince repeated his visit, and was made a brother of different guilds.

Henry VII came to Coventry in 1458, after his victory over Richard III, at Bosworth Field; he lodged at the house of Robert Olney, the Mayor, who presented the King with a cup and £100, and in return was knighted. This King afterwards brought his Queen to see the plays performed by the Grey Friars.

In 1497 Prince Arthur visited the city; he likewise was presented with a cup and £100.

Henry VII and his Queen paid a further visit in 1499, and were made brother and sister of Trinity Guild.

In 1565 Queen Elizabeth visited Coventry, being" splendidly entertained, and when she visited Kenilworth in 1575, she was entertained with the old play of "Hock's Tuesday," performed by inhabitants of the city.

In 1603, Princess Elizabeth, eldest daughter of James I, attended service at St. Michael's Church, and a cup was presented to her at the city's expense. In 1607, James Grant, a native of Coventry, and a notorious conspirator, was executed in London for stealing horses from several gentlemen in the neighbourhood for the purpose of carrying off Princess Elizabeth when on a visit to

Coombe Abbey.

In 1611, Prince Henry, with a train of nobility, came to Coventry, was entertained at St. Mary's Hall, and presented with a purse lined with £50.

In 1687, James II came, was received by the Mayor, and presented with a gold cup weighing 3lbs, and costing no less a sum than £167 7s. 6d.

In 1690, the city was likewise visited by King William, while on his way to Ireland.

The Prince of Wales passed through Coventry in 1807, and Louis XVIII. of France in 1808.

In 1819, Prince Leopold was presented with the freedom of the city.

Queen Adelaide passed through the city on her way to Warwick Castle in 1839.

In 1858, the late Queen Victoria, with Albert, Prince Consort, alighted at Coventry station and drove to Stoneleigh Abbey, being the guest of Lord Leigh, when she visited Warwickshire for the purpose of opening Aston Hall.

In 1874, the Prince and Princess of Wales (afterwards King Edward and Queen Alexandra) visited the city, and were accorded a fitting- reception.

The charter for the annual Great Fair was granted by Henry III in 1218.

In 1406, John Botener caused the streets to be paved.

A ducking stool and pond were made in 1422, with which "to punish scolds and chiders."

In 1446, John Heires and William Lingham were hanged for robbing St. Mary's Hall.

In 1469, a person named Elipane was beheaded, and his head was set on a pole at Bablake Gate; and in 1471, the leaders of an insurrection in London were beheaded at Coventry.

The year 1480 saw a tumult among the inhabitants, and the sword and mace were that year stolen from the Mayor's house.

In 1512, a hundred men were raised in Coventry for foreign service.

In 1522, two men were arrested here for treason, and confessed it was their intention to have put the Mayor and Aldermen to death and to have robbed St. Mary's Hall. They were hanged, drawn, and quartered, and their heads and limbs were exposed on the city gates.

In 1626 two of the City Chamberlains paid a fine of £20 for making a smaller feast at "Lammas" than their predecessors.

Old Parr passed through the city in 1635, at the age of 152 years.

The city was fortified in 1650 against Charles II, and a regiment of infantry raised for its defence.

Weaving was introduced in 1696, and watchmaking about 1710.

In 1711 party spirit ran high in the city, and a plot was made to seize the sword and mace on 1st November, when

John Eburne should go to be sworn as Mayor, at St. Mary's Hall. The sword and mace were, however, deposited in a house in Fleet Street, where, in the open-air, the swearing-in was suddenly gone through.

A case of a woman being burnt to death by supposed spontaneous combustion took place in 1772.

In 1773, Mr. Siddons, the tragedian, was married to Miss Kemble, at St. Michael's Church.

The year 1780 is noted for the "bludgeon fight" at an election between the rival parties, in front of the booth in Cross Cheaping.

In 1800 riots took place owing to the high prices of food.

In 1805 a company of Volunteers was raised here, as was a second company in 1807.

In 1831 Mary Ann Higgins was hanged for poisoning her uncle; and in 1848 Mary Ball suffered the extreme penalty for poisoning her husband at Nuneaton, this being the last execution in Coventry.

In 1842 the New Boundary Act, and in 1844 the Waterworks, Cemetery, and the Coventry Improvement Acts were passed.

The first houses in Chapelfields were erected in 1846.

The Waterworks at Spon End were first put in motion on

September 30th, 1847.

The city was placed under the Public Health Act in 1849.

In 1858 the Great Fair was removed from Grey Friars Green to the Pool Meadow.

In 1860-61 great distress prevailed in the city and neighbourhood, and a relief fund of £40,000 was raised from all parts of the country, the Queen contributing £150, and the Prince of Wales £125.

The cycle industry, introduced a few years earlier, first assumed importance in 1876, though at that time its after proportions were undreamed of.

In 1885, owing to the severe winter and depression of trade, much distress existed in the city. The Corporation, with a view of alleviating the condition of the great numbers of unemployed, organised soup kitchens, and found temporary employment for many in street cleaning and the levelling of Gosford Green.

In 1887 the Jubilee of the Queen was loyally celebrated, while the Diamond Jubilee of 1897 saw Coventry in the very forefront of the national rejoicings.

In January, 1900, the spectacle was witnessed of Coventry citizens turning out in crowds to wish Godspeed and safe return to a detachment of volunteers leaving their homes for the war in South Africa. A couple of months previously, the 77th Battery of Field Artillery, stationed at the Barracks, had likewise left amid similar manifestations of goodwill.

Few that enter the palatial premises and have access to that hive of day and night industry, viz., the Post Ofiice in Hertford Street, can realise that within living memory (December 2nd, 1834), the following order was made at the General Post Office, London: "Ordered, that all letters passing from Coventry to Atherstone, and Atherstone to Coventry, go by Northampton, and that a charge of ninepence postage be made.!'

Parliamentary representation of the city dates from 1295.

The Plague visited the city in 1478, when upwards of 3,000 persons died.

In 1466 Earl Rivers and his son were beheaded outside the city walls.

During the time of the dissolution of religious houses, Coventry suffered much at the hands of the Bishop of Chester, who also caused seven persons to be burned.

The city was visited by Queen Elizabeth, and the beautiful Mary Queen of Scots was at one time confined within its walls as a prisoner.

The city was also visited by Princess Anne of Denmark in 1688, and by King William III in 1690.

The late King Edward VII and Queen Alexandra (then Prince and Princess of Wales) rode through the city after visiting the Earl of Aylesford at Packington Hail in 1874.

In the autumn of 1898 the Duchess of Albany visited Coventry for the purpose of opening a bazaar in connection with St. Thomas' Church. Albany Road, a direct route from the Butts to Earlsdon, was completed about this time, and was so named in commemoration of the visit.

In December, 1899, the Chinese Minister, attended by a numerous suite, spent several days in Coventry while on an "industrial tour" through the country.

On Thursday, July 22nd, 1915, King George V visited Coventry to inspect the production of munitions, and visited some of the industrial establishments. At the Ordnance Works he was informed that 7,462 persons (6,121 men, and 1,341 women), were employed at the Daimler Works 4,750; at Messrs. Alfred Herberts, Ltd., 1,850; and at the Rover Co.'s Works, 1,500. His Majesty, who was loyally received by respectful, yet earnestly demonstrative crowds, expressed regret that his visit was so short, but said he felt most interested in what he had seen, and was convinced that Coventry was going to play her part nobly.

On 26th April, 1911, there died, at the age of 76, Mr. Wm. Bennett, for many years proprietor of the Coventry Theatre Royal, and of its successor the Royal Opera House, in Hales Street, the only place of regular performance of the "legitimate' drama, and a personage well known in the theatrical world.

Richard Baxter (1615-1691), the Puritan divine—who is said to have preached more sermons, engaged in more controversies, and written more books than any other Nonconformist of his age, even preaching within the sound of

cannon when the roll of battle was passing - over Edgehill— was for two years a minister of Coventry.

On the night of Sunday, December 31st, 1900, and the morning of Monday, January 1st, 1901, the River Sherbourne overflowed its banks after an unwonted rainy season, resulting in the most disastrous flood on record. There was witnessed the extraordinary spectacle of boats in the streets. The water rose to a considerable height in hundreds of houses, the inhabitants were driven into the upper storeys, and were there supplied with victuals and drink by kindly disposed persons moving about in carts. St. John's Church was flooded to a height of about six feet.

Amongst men of note connected with the city may be mentioned Vincent of Coventry, who lived in the early part of the 13th century, and was much distinguished for his learning, being a professor at Cambridge, and the author of several theological works; William Macklesfieid, an accomplished scholar and governor of the Order of Dominicans, was a native of Coventry; John Bird, of the Order of the Carmelites here, was appointed Bishop of Bangor and Chester by Henry VIII ; Humphrey Wanley, scholar and antiquarian; John Tippet, the original publisher of the Ladies' Diary in 1704; Mr. Joseph Gutteridge, who died in 1899, an artisan naturalist of considerable repute. All these men were natives of or connected with Coventry, a city that has played no small part in the history of this country, and which has passed through remarkable vicissitudes to its present state of prosperity. It presents an epitome of the history of this country, and to the visitor the strange contrast afforded by its antiquities and the new pulsating life around them, cannot fail to prove most fascinating".

"And Farewell goes out sighing."

Shakespeare.

13492136R00057

Printed in Great Britain
by Amazon